LEARN AGILE & SCRUM IN TWO HOURS

THE ULTIMATE AGILE 101 BOOK FOR BEGINNERS

Luke Pivac & Kieran Morgan

Technical Details

- ISBN: 978-0-9941693-4-1 (paperback); 978-0-9941693-8-9 (e-book)
- Edition: 1st Edition
- Publication Date:
    - Edition 1, Release 1: March 2025
- Authors: Luke Pivac, Kieran Morgan
- Publisher: Boffin Education
- Website: https://boffin.education

Praise for This Book

“Distils what can often feel like an overwhelming and jargon-heavy subject into something both practical and easy to digest.”

Markus Kopco, Principal Program & Project Management Consultant; Certified Scrum Master

“This book does a great job of making Agile easy to understand and keeping it light!”

Bill Raymond, Host of Bill Talks AI

“A really nice introduction to Agile. Covers all the main concepts and doesn’t get sidetracked into focusing on tooling or commercial frameworks.”

Jason Leeming, Head of Portfolio & Governance

Contents

1

About This Book

Introduction

Navigating Agile without sufficient knowledge can feel like finding your way without a compass. To the uninitiated, it can seem like a religion, complete with its own jargon, rituals, and values. Even worse, those who stand against the Agile tide risk being left behind, standing on the shore while others sail forward.

It doesn’t matter whether you’re used to working in traditional waterfall projects or are entirely new to Agile: organizations worldwide are shifting toward a more agile, faster pace of planning, delivering, and executing.

Don't panic. *Learn Agile and Scrum in Two Hours: The Ultimate Agile 101 Book for Beginners* is here to help! This book will teach you the basics of Agile, even if you have zero experience. It will show you what Agile is, how it works, why it's different, and when to use it.

This book is a quick, easy-to-read Agile guide that demystifies key concepts. Whether you’re brand-new to Agile and feel like you’ve been thrown into the deep end, or you’ve only dipped your toes in the Agile waters and want to explore further, this book is for you!

You'll learn the concepts and key terms you need to know to work within an Agile environment. You will discover how Agile differs from traditional methodologies like waterfall and when it's appropriate to use waterfall instead of Agile and vice versa. Plus, you'll learn the Agile values and principles and why they're at the heart of the Agile framework, making it different from other methodologies.

In summary, you will learn:

- The fundamental principles and concepts of Agile.
- How to apply Agile in practice using the Scrum framework, the most common flavor of Agile.
- How to adopt an Agile mindset, with helpful advice for the journey.
- How Agile can help harness the power of productive teamwork to forge high-performing teams.

We've crafted this book using the collective knowledge we've gained as Agile practitioners—all to help you become fluent in Agile in just two hours!

Enjoy reading,

Luke Pivac & Kieran Morgan

Who This Book Is For

Are you new to Agile, or maybe curious about how Agile can help you achieve your goals more effectively? Or have you been thrown into an Agile environment and feel like you're in over your head, drowning in Agile jargon? If you answered yes to any of these questions, this book is for you. It's a simple and clear primer for Agile and Scrum—that you can read in two hours.

This book is for:

- **Agile Beginners** who must do something unfamiliar—Agile—and need a practical, easy guide to follow.
- **Software Developers, Business Analysts, and Testers** who want to see how Agile can improve teamwork and collaboration.
- **Scrum Masters** who need a straightforward reference covering the essentials of Agile and Scrum.
- **Product Owners** who want to clarify their role in guiding the product vision and ensuring customer value.
- **Project Managers** who want to understand how roles like Scrum Master and Product Owner work, so they can transition to an Agile environment.
- **Leaders, Managers, and Executives** who need enough Agile know-how to build and support effective Agile teams—without getting lost in the details.

Why “2 Hours”?

This book is about 16,000 words, and the average reading speed is somewhere in the range of 200–300 words per minute. It should take the average reader about two hours to read this book from cover to cover. But if you need to take more time to study the concepts in depth, please do so!

About the Authors

Luke Pivac

Luke has been leading Agile projects for over 10 years, working with a range of companies from high-tech software firms to major banks. With publications on lukepivac.com and Bookboon, Luke is recognized as a thought leader in the industry who is dedicated to spreading understanding of Agile methodologies and their practical applications.

Luke combines his practical experience of Agile with a deep theoretical understanding. His mission is to help professionals at all levels understand and benefit from Agile practices so they can achieve their full potential.

When not engaged in Agile projects or writing, Luke shares his expertise through workshops, speaking engagements, and one-on-one mentoring. He also spends time with his family in Auckland, New Zealand.

Kieran Morgan

Kieran is a process improvement leader with two decades of experience driving operational excellence, enterprise transformation, and strategic change across corporate and government sectors.

Drawing on Lean Six Sigma, Agile, and business process architecture, he specializes in designing scalable frameworks that turn complexity into clarity.

Kieran holds a Master of Project Management and is a certified Lean Six Sigma Black Belt. His current focus is exploring how systems theory and methodologies like Agile Scrum can enhance decision-making in complex environments.

When he's not optimizing workflows or refining processes, Kieran enjoys spending time with his partner and daughters in Sydney, Australia.

Luke’s Story: Agile’s True Worth in Times of Crisis

When the COVID-19 pandemic hit, everything changed almost overnight. One day, I was collaborating face-to-face with my team in the New Zealand government's health software department; the next, we were all isolated behind screens and trying to make sense of a new remote reality. As a Senior Scrum Master leading our DevOps integration team, I found myself in uncharted territory.

The stakes were higher than ever. We were responsible for critical health software that would support our nation's response to the pandemic. Suddenly, nobody knew what to do. The usual routines and processes seemed inadequate for the challenges we were facing. I realized that this was a moment where Agile principles could truly make a difference—but we'd have to adapt them to fit our new circumstances.

To tackle these challenges, I decided to fully embrace the *Agile Manifesto*. We'd been operating in hybrid mode, afraid to let go of the traditional waterfall methods that were holding us back.

With the team's agreement, we shifted our focus to actionable tasks and timeboxed our efforts to keep the momentum going. Documentation took a backseat to action lists, allowing us to respond swiftly to changing needs. Instead of leading from the top, I found myself doing more bottom-up leadership—taking notes during our big meetings, capturing decisions on the fly, and making sure we followed up promptly.

Without the old constraints holding us back, we were free to try new techniques and focus on the most important thing: delivering value to the customer. Despite the hurdles, we successfully navigated the chaos by embracing Agile principles. Our senior leadership quickly noticed our performance and praised the critical role we played in maintaining operations and emotionally supporting each other during such stressful times.

Leading a 30-member remote Scrumban team during lockdown was one of the most challenging yet educational experiences of my career. This journey taught me the true value of Agile—not just as a methodology, but as a mindset. It reinforced my belief that with trust, collaboration, and adaptability, teams can overcome any obstacle. This experience is the foundation of my ability to help you, and your teams reach new heights.

How to Use This Book

You don't have to follow every step or read every page. The bitesize format of this book allows you to take it at your own pace, skipping anything that isn't relevant to you.

Symbols Used in This Book

While reading this book, you'll encounter reader aids, which are easily identifiable by their accompanying symbols. The following table explains the purpose of each.

Table 1: Symbols Used in This Book

(lightbulb)	**Insight:** Insights offer an extra dimension to the guidance provided in this book. They may suggest career-enhancing moves, sound notes of caution, or shed additional light on a concept.
(magnifying glass)	**What Does That Mean?** Definitions for technical jargon used in the accompanying text. All definitions are compiled in the glossary.
(clipboard)	**Note:** Additional information about a concept or section that is not essential for understanding but provides more context.

Acknowledgements

Luke and Kieran extend their heartfelt thanks to everyone who contributed their time and effort to this project. A special thanks to our partners and families for their patience and support as we spent countless early mornings, evenings, and weekends refining this book—we couldn't have done it without you.

To Steve Moss—your time, commitment, and unwavering support have been invaluable. Your contributions have enriched this book in ways we can't thank you enough for.

To Katherine Colina (Kieran's partner)—an enormous thank you for your support and for giving me the time and space to bring this project to life. I hope this book proves helpful on your own IT journey!

To our brilliant expert reviewers: Kym Mawson-Lee, Beth Gervase, Markus Kopco, Bill Raymond, James Gorman, and Jason Leeming. Thank you for lending your considerable Agile experience to this project, reviewing our drafts, providing loads of helpful feedback, and making this guide so much better!

2

Agile Concepts

Introduction

Agile is all about flexibility and continuous improvement. While the *Agile Manifesto* was written in 2001, the ideas behind Agile—like working in small steps and adapting as you go—have been around for decades.

What makes Agile different from traditional project management (like waterfall) is its approach to change. Instead of seeing change as a disruption, Agile teams expect it, plan for it, and even welcome it.

Rather than spending months (or years) mapping out every detail before getting started, Agile teams plan just enough to move forward, adjusting as they learn more. This is called "just-in-time planning," and it keeps projects from getting bogged down by rigid structures.

Agile frameworks—such as Scrum—work in short, focused cycles, usually called sprints, where teams regularly review progress and make improvements. The goal isn't to follow a process but to deliver something valuable as quickly and efficiently as possible.

What Does That Mean?

Just in Time (JIT) Planning: An iterative approach where stakeholders and teams work together to complete a project, planning just enough—a few steps ahead.

Sprint: Timeboxed intervals of work (typically two weeks) characteristic of the Agile Scrum framework.

What Is Agile?

Agile is a flexible, iterative approach to project management and product development that prioritizes adaptability, collaboration, and continuous value delivery. Agile frameworks help teams break work into short, focused cycles called sprints, typically lasting two to four weeks, allowing for faster feedback and incremental improvements.

Instead of waiting months (or even years) to see results, Agile teams deliver progress in small, usable increments. At the end of each sprint, the team releases a working feature or product update—something customers can use, test, and provide feedback on. This ongoing feedback loop helps teams refine priorities, adjust scope, and pivot direction when needed, ensuring the project stays aligned with real-world customer needs.

But Agile isn't just about speed—it's about adaptability. Teams can quickly respond to change, continuously improve their work, and keep customers engaged throughout the process.

More than just a process, Agile is a mindset and philosophy—one that values collaboration, feedback, and flexibility over rigid plans, heavy documentation, and fixed contracts. It's about delivering what truly matters, not just ticking boxes.

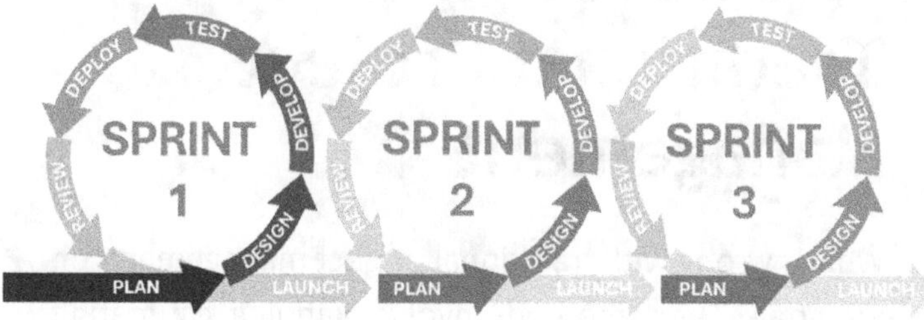

Figure 1: The Agile Scrum Process and Iterative Sprints

What Does That Mean?

Agile: A project management and product development philosophy that emphasizes iterative progress, adaptability, and continuous value delivery.

Agile Framework: A structured approach that applies Agile principles through defined roles, workflows, and practices to help teams deliver value efficiently. Examples include Scrum, Kanban, Extreme Programming (XP), and Lean.

The Issues with Traditional Project Management

What's wrong with traditional project management, or waterfall? Those methods involve planning, estimating, and documenting a complete solution up front—before any of the actual build work begins. Once the work does begin, tasks are actioned in a series of sequential stages.

Just like a waterfall cascading from one tier to the next, it can never repeat the previous step. Not without a lot of costly variations, anyway!

While this sequential process seems logical and straightforward, it can cause major issues during digital and software development projects. We'll explore these issues next.

What Does That Mean?

Waterfall: The traditional linear project delivery framework. It involves planning, estimating, and documenting a complete solution up front. Its cascading process is like a waterfall, hence the term.

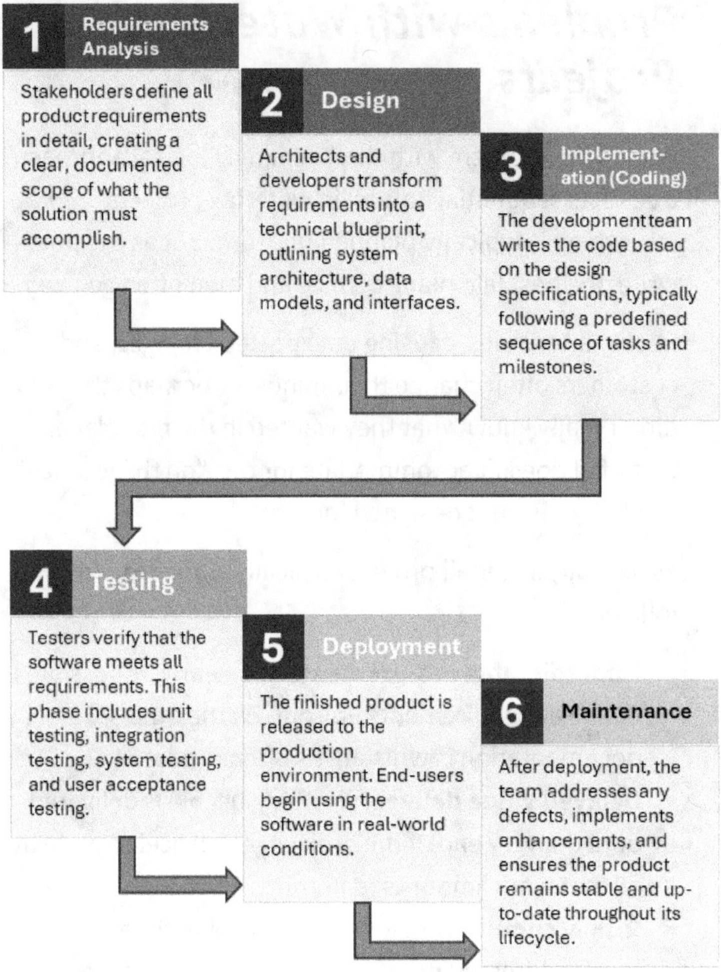

Figure 2: Typical Waterfall Process

Problems with Waterfall Projects

What's the problem with this seemingly logical approach? Due to its sequential nature, in waterfall projects, everything is typically planned up-front. But as the poets write, the best laid plans of mice and men often go awry.

Reality intervenes, causing unexpected changes, and customers often change their minds, or perhaps they didn't really know what they wanted in the first place. Waterfall doesn't accommodate for this "on the journey" flexibility—it's not designed for that.

As a result, waterfall projects typically suffer from the following:

- **Unpredictable requirements:** It's nearly impossible to define all requirements upfront. By the time documentation is written, it's often outdated.
- **Delayed value delivery:** Nothing usable is delivered until the very end. If the project gets canceled midway, all that work amounts to nothing.
- **Risk accumulation:** Risks build up over time instead of being addressed iteratively, making them harder to manage.
- **Rigidity:** Changes are seen as disruptions rather than opportunities, leading to friction between customers and teams and ultimately impacting quality.

Because modern software environments (and many other fields) evolve so rapidly, waterfall's linear nature can struggle to keep pace, often leaving teams with outdated requirements or unsatisfactory products.

That said, waterfall is still widely used—and sometimes even required—in places where altering the plan mid-project is prohibitively complex or costly. We'll explore these scenarios in the section, "When *Isn't* Agile Suitable?" on page 148, to show how waterfall continues to be the standard in certain contexts.

Agile Manifesto

By the late 1990s, many software professionals were frustrated with the rigid, heavily documented, and sequential nature of the waterfall method—the dominant approach in large-scale software projects.

Waterfall's step-by-step structure left little room for change, yet software development is naturally dynamic. Customers often refined their needs mid-project, market conditions shifted, and new technologies emerged.

A group of 17 software practitioners, already experimenting with more flexible approaches, gathered in 2001 to define a shared philosophy. Their goal was to prioritize collaboration, adaptability, and customer satisfaction over rigid documentation and process-heavy management.

Instead of a strict methodology, they outlined a set of values and principles to guide software teams, publishing them as the *Agile Manifesto* (Beck, et al. 2001).

The impact was enormous. Agile became the dominant approach to software development, influencing not just software teams but project management, product development, and even business operations. Over twenty years since the *Manifesto* was published, Agile adoption surged to 86% among software development teams, according to consultancy Digital.ai (Digital.ai 2021).

If you read the *Agile Manifesto*, two things stand out:

1. **It's remarkably concise.** In just 68 words, it defines four key values and twelve supporting principles.
2. **It's based on values, not rigid rules.** This flexibility is a key reason why Agile has flourished—it's a mindset as much as a methodology.

What Does That Mean?

Agile Manifesto: A foundational document for software development expressing the core values and principles that inform Agile ways of working created in 2001 by 17 software experts.

Agile Values

Agile values shape the culture, mindset, and work practices of Agile teams. Instead of rigidly following bureaucratic processes that may or may not produce meaningful results, Agile teams prioritize delivering value to customers in a flexible and adaptive way.

The *Agile Manifesto* defines four core values:

- Individuals and interactions over processes and tools
- Working software over comprehensive documentation
- Customer collaboration over contract negotiation
- Responding to change over following a plan

It's important to note that the items on the right still have value. Agile doesn't eliminate planning, documentation, or contracts—but it prioritizes people, adaptability, and working solutions over rigid adherence to rules.

These values are central to Agile's success. Agile isn't just a bunch of frameworks like Scrum and the Scale Agile Framework (SAFe)—it's a mindset that helps teams navigate an ever-changing, complex world. By emphasizing collaboration, continuous improvement, and customer feedback, Agile provides a flexible alternative to traditional, plan-driven project management.

Insight: Adopting Agile Values

Teams who adopt Agile values often feel more empowered, engaged, and passionate about their work, as they have more autonomy, ownership, and alignment with the project vision and goals. According to consultancy JCURV, 71% of employees in Agile organizations with 1,001–5,000 staff feel empowered by their leadership, and that number rises to 86% for organizations with over 20,000 employees (JCURV 2020).

What Does That Mean?

Agile Values: The core beliefs that guide Agile philosophy, such as prioritizing individuals and interactions over processes and tools, working software over comprehensive documentation, customer collaboration over contract negotiation, and responding to change over following a plan.

Individuals and Interactions over Processes and Tools

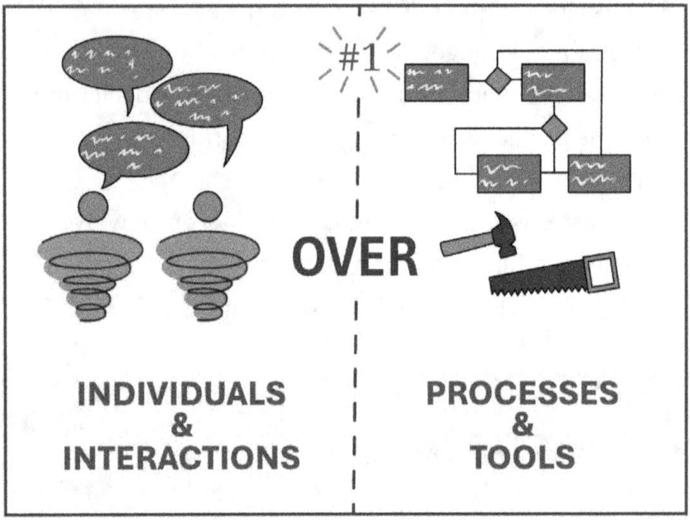

Figure 3: Individuals and Interactions over Processes and Tools

Agile emphasizes the importance of teamwork and collaboration over rigid processes and tools. Unlike traditional methods that often result in bureaucratic behaviors, such as slavish adherence to process—even if this results in terrible outcomes! —Agile recognizes that engaging with people is more important. By valuing individuals and interactions over processes and tools, Agile fosters an environment where innovation is not only encouraged, it thrives.

Working Software over Comprehensive Documentation

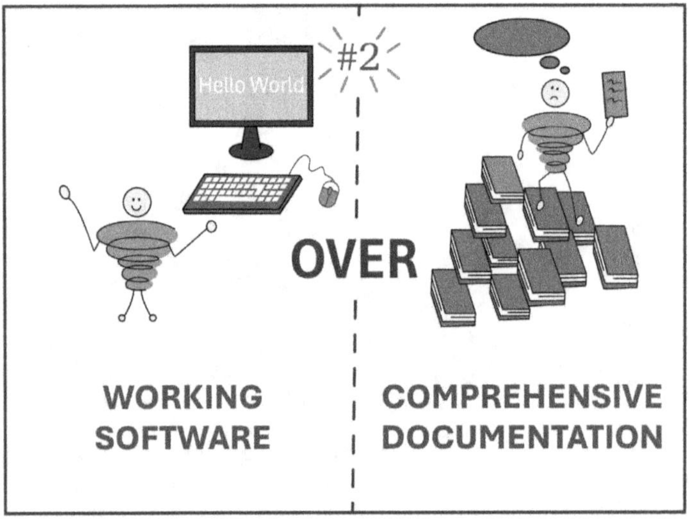

Figure 4: Working Software over Comprehensive Documentation

Agile prioritizes delivering functional software that meets customer needs over creating extensive documentation. This doesn't mean documentation is unnecessary, but it should be limited to what is useful and necessary. In software development projects, minimal manuals or guides are usually all that are needed, though some projects still require comprehensive user guides or training materials. While Agile reduces the emphasis on detailed specifications compared to waterfall, documents like test specifications remain essential to ensure quality standards. The main goal is to avoid excessive and quickly outdated documentation.

Table 2: Do’s and Don'ts of Agile Documentation

Do's	Don'ts
✓ Focus on delivering functional software	✗ Produce excessive documentation that doesn't add value
✓ Create documentation when necessary and useful	✗ Prioritize detailed specs over actual working software
✓ Ensure user documentation is clear and minimal	✗ Create large, complex manuals if the software is intuitive
✓ Maintain essential documentation for quality standards	✗ Skip necessary documentation for testing and delivery

Customer Collaboration over Contract Negotiation

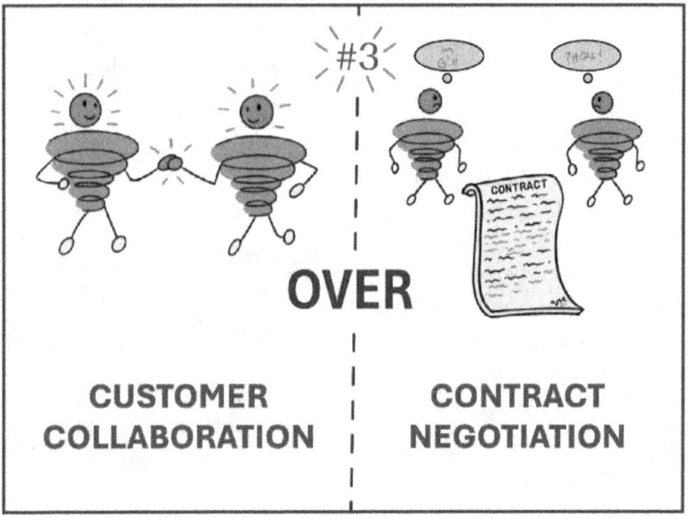

Figure 5: Customer Collaboration over Contract Negotiation

Traditional project management often relies on contract negotiation, which means fixing scope, schedule, and budget up front. It can create an antagonistic relationship, where everyone tries to do the minimum expected of them under the contract in an attempt to maximize their own benefit, chiefly financial. As you can imagine, this doesn't lead to great results.

Agile, however, emphasizes *customer value* over contract negotiation. It does so by making customer collaboration, regular communication, feedback, and alignment key focuses. This creates a partnership arrangement where everyone benefits by working together to create the best possible products and often creating mutually beneficial long-term relationships.

What Does That Mean?

Customer Value: The benefit a product delivers to its users. In other words, how well does the software (or solution) meet customer needs and solve their problems?

Responding to Change over Following a Plan

Figure 6: Responding to Change over Following a Plan

Agile emphasizes adapting quickly and flexibly to change rather than sticking to a detailed plan. To be Agile, you must be pragmatic—change is inevitable! By planning only as much as necessary (just-in-time planning), teams can adjust to change when it occurs, whether it's from evolving requirements or an unexpected change in circumstances.

Agile projects do involve planning, but it's an ongoing process. Agile plans are living documents that evolve with stakeholder needs and feedback. They focus on the immediate future and are frequently revised based on each sprint's outcomes.

Agile's Principles-Based Approach

The *Agile Manifesto* advocates a principles-based approach. This makes it very flexible and responsive to customer needs. In contrast, traditional approaches provide best practices: steps, processes, competencies, and knowledge areas that project managers are expected to master to effectively deliver projects.

These best practices—which have been accumulated by generations of project managers—are assumed to achieve good outcomes. However, understanding how to apply these best practices effectively can take decades to master. Even worse, these traditional methods assume that the best practices are suitable for all scenarios or that the project manager using them is experienced enough to understand where they need to be adapted.

However, projects are rarely one-size-fits-all—and highly experienced project managers don't grow on trees! This isn't just true for software development, it's true of many projects. A principles-based approach, such as Agile, allows for creativity, collaboration, and experimentation, as well as continuous improvement and learning.

A principles-based approach enables the project team and stakeholders to work together to deliver the best possible solution rather than following a predetermined plan or specification—and as it's a team-based approach it doesn't rely on a single, brilliant individual to orchestrate it, such as the Scrum Master.

Here are the two most common traditional approaches:

Table 3: Project Management Methods

Process-Based Approaches	**Knowledge-Area Based Approaches**
A process-based approach, such as Projects in Controlled Environments (PRINCE2), prescribes a set of sequential steps and activities that must be followed for project management regardless of the context or the nature of the project. In PRINCE2, this process is orchestrated by the project manager.	A knowledge-area based approach, such as the Project Management Institute (PMI)'s *Project Management Body of Knowledge* (PMBOK), defines a set of domains and competencies that project managers need to master to successfully deliver projects—but leaves it up to the project manager to figure out how to do so. As in PRINCE2, in PMBOK, this process is orchestrated by the project manager.

Agile's Twelve Principles

The *Agile Manifesto* identifies twelve guiding principles that build on and expand the concepts embodied in the Agile values. These principles will help you understand how to "operationalize" the Agile values in your work. Embrace them as part of your Agile journey from being a newcomer to becoming a skilled team player in a high-performing Agile team.

The twelve principles are listed on the following page and can also be found on the *Agile Manifesto* website.

What Does That Mean?

Agile Principles: Guiding principles that build on and expand the concepts embodied in the Agile values, facilitating the development of an Agile mindset and work practices.

Agile's twelve principles:

1. Our highest priority is to satisfy the customer through early and continuous delivery of valuable software.
2. Welcome changing requirements, even late in development. Agile processes harness change for the customer's competitive advantage.
3. Deliver working software frequently, from a couple of weeks to a couple of months, with a preference to the shorter timescale.
4. Business people and developers must work together daily throughout the project.
5. Build projects around motivated individuals. Give them the environment and support they need and trust them to get the job done.
6. The most efficient and effective method of conveying information to and within a Development Team is face-to-face conversation.
7. Working software is the primary measure of progress.
8. Agile processes promote sustainable development. The sponsors, developers, and users should be able to maintain a constant pace indefinitely.
9. Continuous attention to technical excellence and good design enhances agility.
10. Simplicity—the art of maximizing the amount of work not done—is essential.
11. The best architecture, requirements, and designs emerge from self-organizing teams.
12. At regular intervals, the team reflects on how to become more effective, then tunes and adjusts its behavior accordingly.

Agile Frameworks

Agile is an overarching set of values and principles—a guiding philosophy for working more collaboratively, efficiently, iteratively, and flexibly on projects to deliver better outcomes. But how do you actually "do" Agile? Like traditional project methodologies such as PMBOK, the *Agile Manifesto* is fantastic at telling you *what* and *why*—but not so much *how* to apply it.

That brings us to Agile frameworks. Frameworks are a set of practices and tools that help teams and enterprises apply Agile values and principles in their projects. Agile frameworks provide advice on how to plan, execute, and deliver products or services in a way that aligns with the spirit and intention of the Agile values and principles. They're customizable to suit different situations and needs, and they provide the essential "how" that's missing from a high-level manifesto.

The most commonly used Agile frameworks are Scrum, Kanban, Scaled Agile Framework (SAFe), and Scrumban—a combination of Scrum and Kanban. Scrum is by far the most common Agile framework at the team level: according to consultancy Digital.ai, Scrum is used by 63% of Agile users (Digital.ai 2023).

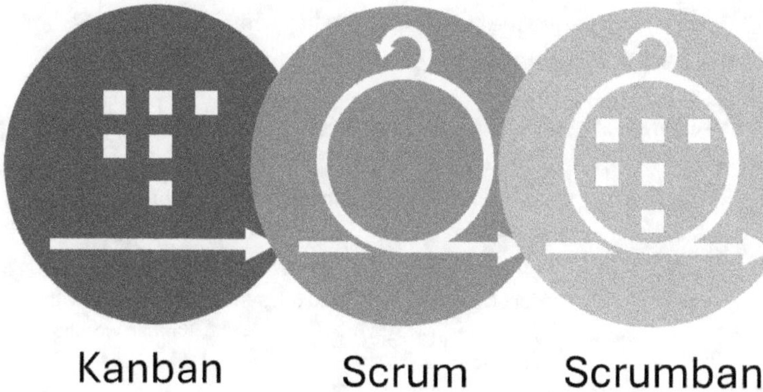

Figure 7: Kanban, Scrum, and Scrumban

What Does That Mean?

Kanban: An Agile framework that emphasizes lean principles such as continuous delivery, a pull-based workflow system, limiting work in progress, and visualizing workflow with a Kanban board.

Scrum: An iterative and lightweight Agile software development framework. It focuses on small teams of people working together with highly specified roles to address complex problems, incrementally deliver value, and continuously improve.

Scrumban: A hybrid Agile framework that blends the structure and discipline of Scrum with the flexibility and flow of Kanban.

Table 4: Comparing the Most Popular Agile Team Frameworks: Scrum, Kanban, and Scrumban

Feature	Scrum	Kanban	Scrumban
Approach	Iterative and incremental	Continuous flow	Hybrid of Scrum and Kanban
Roles	Product Owner, Scrum Master, Development Team	No fixed roles	Scrum roles with Kanban workflow
Workflow	Time-boxed sprints (usually 2-4 weeks)	Continuous delivery, pull-based system	Uses Scrum iterations with Kanban flow and WIP limits
Planning	Sprint planning at the start of each sprint	Planning is continuous, done as needed	Combines Sprint Planning with continuous planning
Meetings	Daily stand-ups, Sprint Reviews, Retrospectives	Meetings as needed; no specific meetings mandated	Daily stand-ups, reviews Retrospectives as needed
Focus	Delivering a potentially shippable product increment	Visualizing and managing workflow, limiting WIP	Delivering value through continuous improvement
Best For	Complex projects needing defined roles and structure	Projects requiring flexibility and continuous delivery	Teams needing a balance of structure and flexibility

3

Agile Process

Introduction

While the *Agile Manifesto* outlines the “what” and “why” through its values and principles, the Agile process represents the “how,” providing a structured yet flexible approach to achieving these values. Frameworks like Scrum and Kanban offer specific practices and tools to implement the Agile process effectively.

The Agile process, regardless of the specific framework used, generally follows a series of iterative and incremental phases. It’s these phases that we’re going to talk about here. They include planning, design, development, testing, deployment, review, and launch. Each iteration, or sprint, in an Agile framework like Scrum involves repeating these phases to produce a functional “increment” of the product.

Then the entire process is repeated as many times as necessary.

Note

There’s no single, universal version of the Agile process; each organization adapts the core ideas to fit its needs, whether through Scrum, Kanban, or a hybrid method. However, in most medium to large organizations, you’ll find a broadly similar, iterative and incremental workflow that covers these phases.

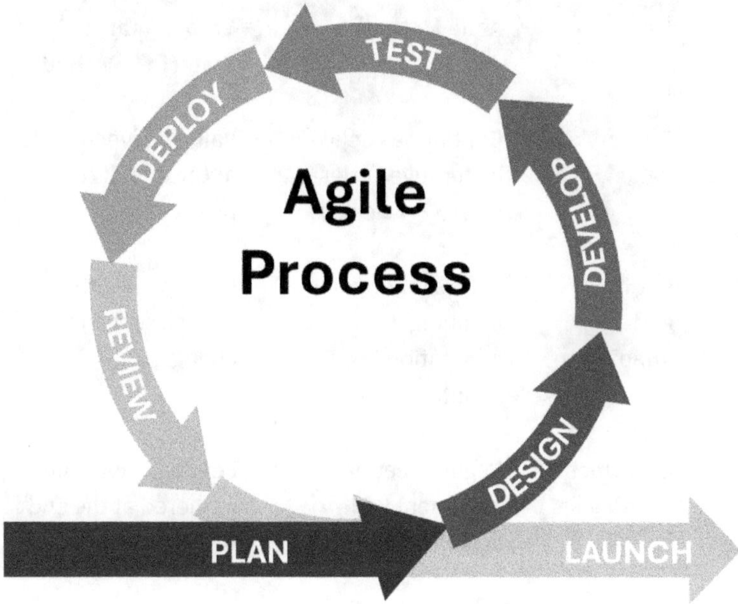

Figure 8: Phases of the Agile Process

This iterative, cyclical approach ensures continuous value delivery of working product components or features to customers every two to four weeks—the usual length of a sprint. The process gives Agile an advantage over traditional methods where value is only delivered at the end of the project.

Let's look at the advantages of Agile over traditional methods in Table 5.

Table 5: Advantages of Agile vs Traditional Methods

Aspect	Agile Method	Traditional Waterfall Method
Delivery of Value	Continuous delivery in iterative cycles (every 2-4 weeks)	Value delivered only at the end of the project
Flexibility and Adaptation	Allows for ongoing planning and adaptation in each sprint	Fixed plan with limited scope for changes
Customer Feedback	Regular feedback and alignment with stakeholders	Feedback typically gathered at the end of the project
Project Phases	Iterative and incremental phases (planning, design, development, testing, deployment, review, launch)	Linear and sequential phases (planning, design, development, testing, deployment, launch)
Response to Change	Agile teams can pivot and adapt quickly to changes	Changes are difficult to implement and may cause delays
Customer Satisfaction	High due to continuous delivery and adaptation	Can be low if final product does not meet expectations

The Agile Process

The Agile process is an iterative approach to software development and project management that emphasizes flexibility, collaboration, and customer satisfaction. This cycle includes planning, designing, developing, testing, deploying, reviewing, and launching.

Key outputs at each stage include user stories, wireframes, product increments, testing results, deployment plans, and stakeholder feedback.

The Agile process fosters continuous improvement and ensures efficient project delivery that meets the evolving needs of customers and stakeholders. This table provides a bird's-eye view of the Agile process at a glance.

Table 6: Agile Process at a Glance

Phase	Activities	Outputs
Plan	Define scope, goals, requirements, roles, and responsibilities.	User Stories, Product Backlog, Tasks
Design	Communicate ideas, validate assumptions, gather feedback.	Wireframes, Mock-ups, Prototypes
Develop	Build and integrate the software product.	Potentially Shippable Product Increment (PSI), Codebase
Test	Verify and validate quality and functionality.	Unit Testing, System Testing, User Acceptance Testing (UAT), Performance Testing
Deploy	Release the software to staging or production environment.	Deployment Plan, Release Notes, Deployment Scripts
Review	Evaluate results, measure success criteria (performance, satisfaction).	Sprint Review, Retrospective Report, Stakeholder Feedback
Launch	Celebrate completion, recognize team efforts, and conduct closure activities.	Marketing Materials, User Documentation, Support Plan

Plan

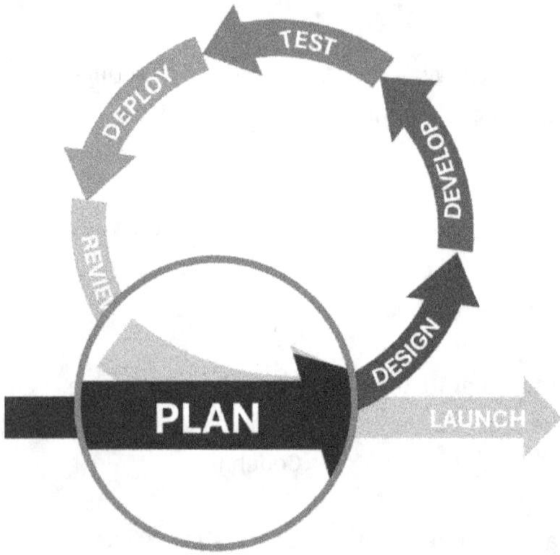

Figure 9: The Plan Phase of the Agile Process

In Agile, planning typically happens at two levels:

1. **Project-Level Planning**: Early on, the team lays the foundation by clarifying the overall goals, scope, and vision for the project. This is where high-level requirements are gathered, roles and responsibilities are established, and the big picture of what needs to be built is formed.

2. **Sprint-Level (Iteration) Planning**: Once the broader vision is set, the team plans each iteration or sprint. Here, they decide which User Stories—the high-level features or functionalities—will move from the Product Backlog into the sprint for development. These user stories are then broken down into smaller, more manageable Tasks that can be completed within the sprint timeframe.

Because Agile welcomes changing requirements, planning is continuous—teams revisit these levels whenever the customer's needs evolve or new insights arise.

Outputs of the Plan Phase:

- **User Stories:** Short, simple descriptions of a feature or functionality from the perspective of the end user, written in a way that captures the who, what, and why.
- **Product Backlog:** A prioritized list of all user stories and tasks that the team will work on throughout the project.
- **Tasks:** The specific, actionable steps that need to be completed to fulfill a user story. Tasks break down user stories into smaller, more manageable pieces of work that can be assigned to team members and completed within a sprint.

Design

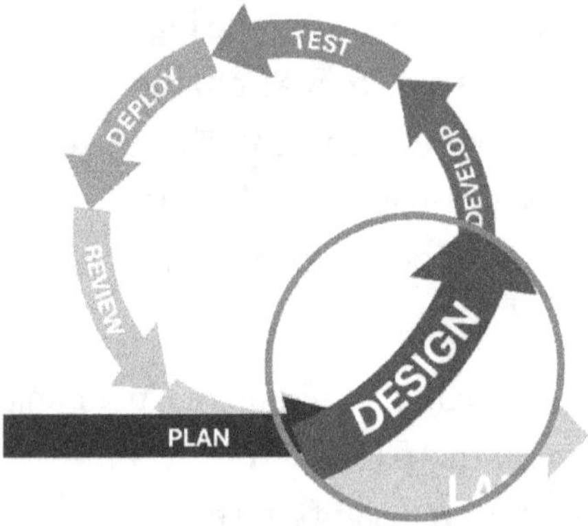

Figure 10: The Design Phase of the Agile Process

The design phase focuses on creating visual representations of the software solution, such as wireframes, mock-ups, or prototypes.

This phase helps the team communicate its ideas effectively, validate assumptions early on, and gather feedback from customers and stakeholders.

By visualizing the product, the team can also identify potential technical challenges or risks before development begins, ensuring that any issues are addressed early in the process.

Outputs of the Design Phase:

- **Wireframes:** Basic layouts that outline the structure and functionality of the software without detailing the visual design.
- **Mock-ups:** Detailed visual designs that show how the final product will look and feel, including colors, typography, and imagery.
- **Prototypes:** Interactive models of the software that simulate user interaction, allowing for early testing and feedback.

Develop

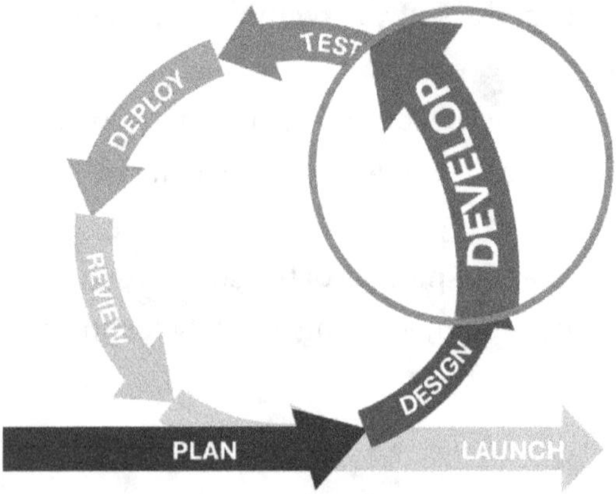

Figure 11: The Develop Phase of the Agile Process

The development phase is where the coding and initial testing take place. The team begins to build and integrate the software product based on the user stories and tasks outlined during the planning phase.

In each sprint, the team focuses on delivering a potentially shippable product increment: a working version of the software that incorporates the features or functionalities completed during that sprint. The team participates in daily Scrum “events” where they discuss their progress, address challenges, and plan their work for the next day. This helps make sure that they’re on track and that everyone agrees with the work that needs to be done.

Outputs of the Development Phase:

- **Potentially Shippable Product Increment (PSI):** A functional, tested version of the software that includes the new features or improvements made during the sprint.
- **Codebase:** The cumulative code that has been developed and integrated, reflecting the progress of the project.

What Does That Mean?

Events: Time-boxed activities (often called "ceremonies") that give Scrum its rhythm. They provide regular opportunities for the team to plan, inspect, adapt, and deliver value. Standard Scrum events include the Sprint, Sprint Planning, the Daily Scrum, the Sprint Review, and the Sprint Retrospective.

Test

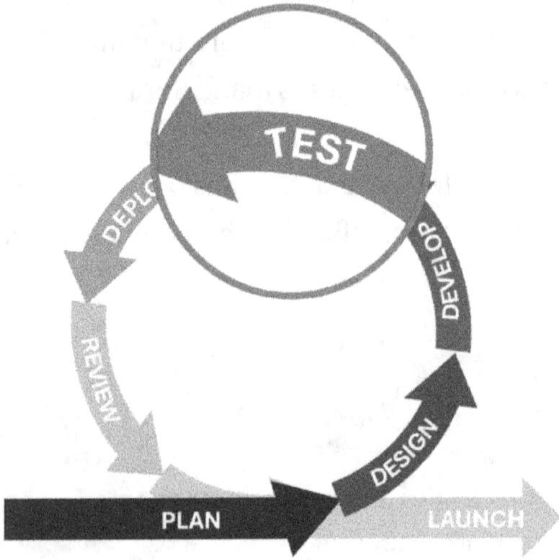

Figure 12: The Test Phase of the Agile Process

The testing phase involves verifying and validating the quality and functionality of the product. It's a critical phase: it ensures that any issues or bugs in the product are fixed before it's released.

In Agile, different types of tests and tools are used.

What Does That Mean?

Nonfunctional Requirements: Define how the software should execute the functional requirements. Non-functional requirements relate to the software's quality and performance, such as speed, reliability, etc.

Outputs of the Test Phase:

- **Unit Testing**: Test components of software to check if they work as expected and follow the design specifications. Detect and fix errors early in the development process.
- **System Testing**: Test the entire software system as a single entity to verify if it meets the functional and non-functional requirements. Evaluate the software's behavior and performance under different scenarios and conditions.
- **User Acceptance Testing (UAT)**: Test the software with the customers to validate if it meets their needs.
- **Performance Testing**: Test the software's speed, responsiveness, stability, scalability, and reliability under various environments. Measure and improve the software's efficiency and quality.
- **Deployment**: The process of making the software available for use in a production environment. This includes packaging the software, configuring the production environment, and transferring the software from a test environment to production.

Deploy

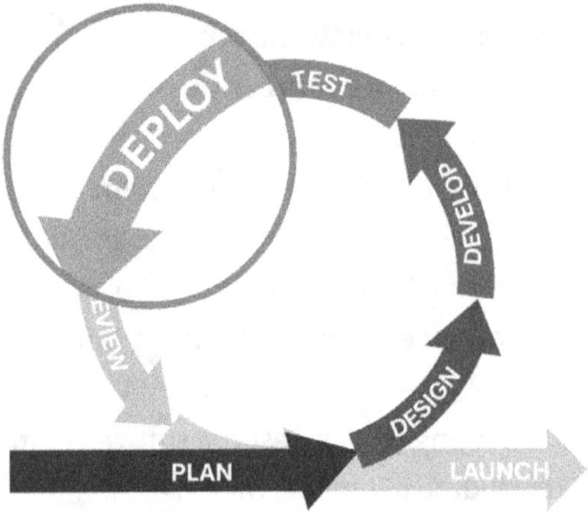

Figure 13: The Deploy Phase of the Agile Process

The deployment phase involves releasing the software solution to customers, often either in a staging or a production environment, depending on your organization's needs. This phase ensures that the software is ready for use and that it can be installed, configured, and maintained easily and securely. Deployment often involves providing documentation, training, and support to customers, as well as monitoring and troubleshooting any issues that may arise after the release.

Outputs of the Deploy Phase:

- **Deployment Plan:** A comprehensive plan outlining the steps, resources, and timeline required to deploy the software to the production environment.
- **Release Notes:** Documentation that provides an overview of the new features, improvements, and bug fixes included in the release.
- **Deployment Scripts:** Automated scripts used to deploy the software to the production environment, ensuring consistency and reducing the risk of errors.

What Does That Mean?

Staging Environment: A replica of the production environment where the software can be tested and evaluated before it is released to the customer. The staging environment allows the team to get feedback from the customer and make any changes or improvements before the final release.

Production Environment: The actual environment where the software runs and operates for the customer. The staging environment helps to ensure that the software meets the quality and functionality requirements and that there are no bugs or errors in the production environment.

Review

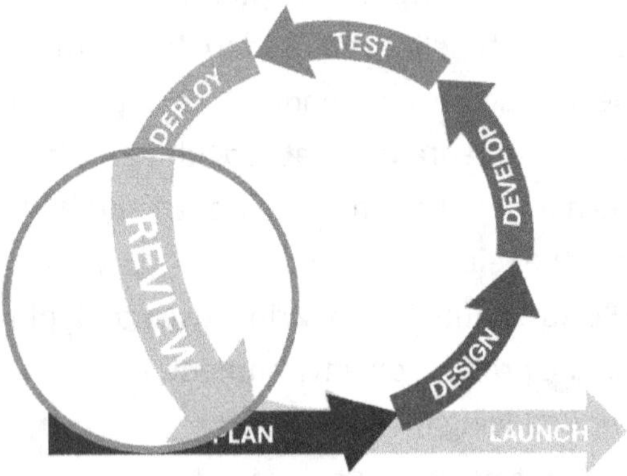

Figure 14: The Review Phase of the Agile Process

The review phase involves evaluating and measuring the results and outcomes of the project to date, as well as the performance and satisfaction of the team, stakeholders, and customers. This phase helps the team to identify the strengths and weaknesses of the project, as well as the lessons learned and best practices that can be applied to future projects. The review phase involves gathering and analyzing feedback from customers, as well as conducting surveys, interviews, or focus groups to assess how well the stakeholders' expectations were met not just throughout the project, but also at the end.

Outputs of the Review Phase:

- **Sprint Review:** A meeting where the team demonstrates the potentially shippable product increment to stakeholders and gathers feedback.
- **Retrospective Report:** A summary of the team's reflections on the sprint, including what went well, what could be improved, and actionable steps for future sprints.
- **Stakeholder Feedback:** Input and suggestions from stakeholders regarding the product increment and overall project progress.

Launch

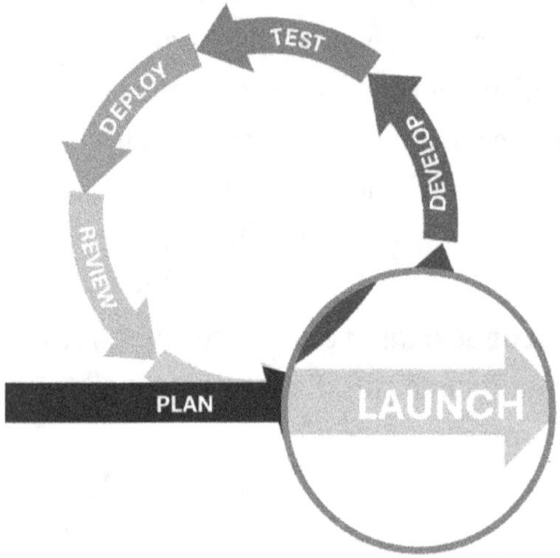

Figure 15: The Launch Phase of the Agile Process

The launch phase involves celebrating the completion and success of the project, as well as recognizing and rewarding the efforts and achievements of the team. This phase also includes transferring the ownership and responsibility of the software or service to the stakeholders and customers, as well as closing the project and releasing the team working on the project.

Outputs of the Launch Phase:

- **Marketing Materials**: Promotional content, such as press releases, blog posts, and social media updates, to announce the launch of the software.
- **User Documentation:** Guides, tutorials, and FAQs to help users understand and effectively use the software.
- **Support Plan:** A plan outlining the resources and processes in place to provide ongoing support and address any issues that arise post-launch.

4

Agile Practice

Introduction

Agile is more than a philosophy—it's a practical approach to delivering value in a structured yet flexible way. While different Agile frameworks (such as Scrum and Kanban) offer their own methods, a common set of core practices has emerged. These practices help teams stay aligned, manage work effectively, and respond to change with minimal disruption.

At its core, Agile succeeds because it prioritizes adaptability, collaboration, and continuous improvement. To make this work in practice, teams need structured ways to:

- Break down and managing work efficiently.
- Ensure clarity on when tasks are ready to start and when they are truly complete.
- Measure progress and maintain a sustainable pace.
- Continuously refine what they are working on based on feedback and evolving needs.

In this chapter, we'll explore the key Agile practices that support these goals, starting with how work is structured—from high-level vision and epics down to user stories and tasks.

We'll examine the role of Acceptance Criteria, Definition of Done, and Definition of Ready in maintaining quality and alignment, as well as how teams use Velocity to measure progress and improve predictability. Finally, we'll discuss the importance of Backlog Refinement in keeping priorities clear and ensuring work flows smoothly.

Breaking Down Agile Requirements

Agile thrives on adaptability, but successful teams still need a structured approach to managing work. Instead of trying to plan everything in one go, Agile teams break down requirements into manageable layers—from big-picture goals to detailed tasks. This structured breakdown ensures clarity, alignment, and flexibility throughout the development process.

At every level of an Agile project, work is structured to ensure a clear flow from strategy to execution. Below is a breakdown of how Agile teams manage requirements, moving from high-level objectives to detailed tasks.

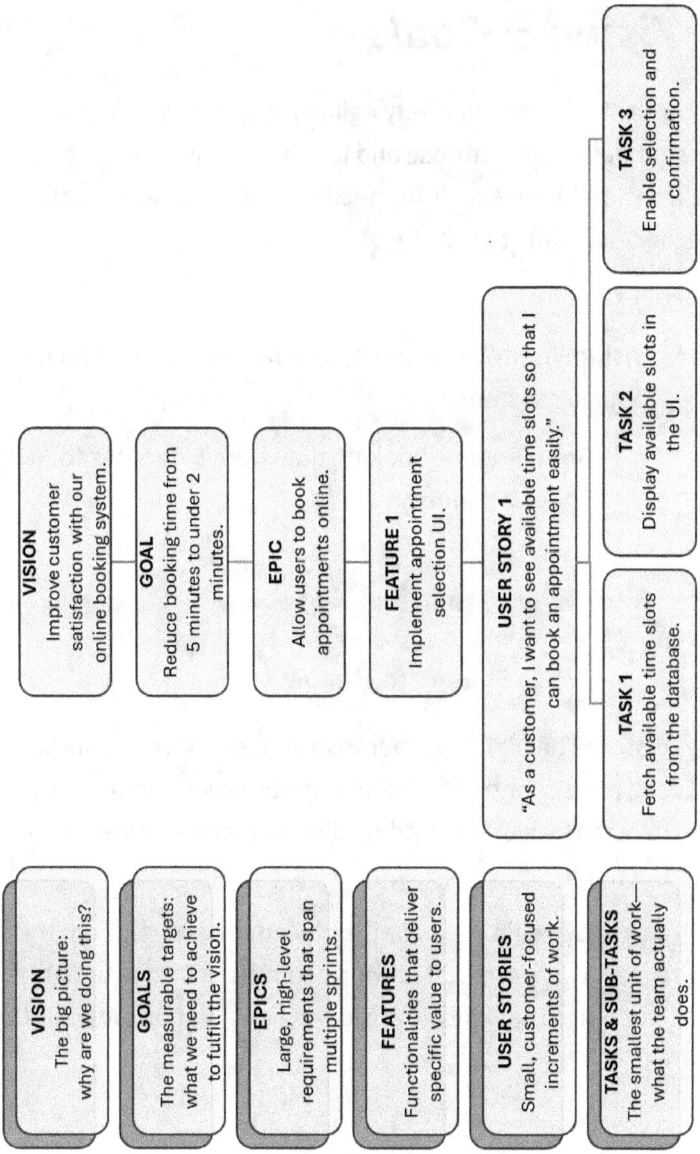

Figure 16: Agile Requirements Breakdown

Vision & Goals

At the highest level, every Agile project starts with a vision that defines its purpose and long-term objectives. Goals translate this vision into specific business outcomes that the team aims to achieve.

For example:

- **Vision:** Improve customer satisfaction with our online booking system.
    - **Goal:** Reduce booking time from 5 minutes to under 2 minutes.

What Does That Mean?

Vision: The high-level purpose and long-term aspiration of a project or product. It defines the overarching "why" behind the work, providing direction and inspiration for the team.

Goals: Specific, measurable objectives derived from the vision. Goals translate broad aspirations into actionable outcomes that guide decision-making and prioritization.

Epics

An epic is a substantial piece of work that represents a major user need or business capability. Epics are too big to be tackled in a single sprint, so they are broken down into smaller deliverables.

For example:

- **Epic:** Allow users to book appointments online.

What Does That Mean?

Epics: Large, high-level requirements that represent major user needs or business capabilities, often spanning multiple sprints.

Features

A feature is a concrete capability that contributes to the epic. While an epic describes the broader need, features represent specific components that will bring that need to life.

For example:

- **Feature:** Enable users to select available time slots.

What Does That Mean?

Features: Specific functionalities that deliver value to the user and contribute to fulfilling an epic.

Note

The exact hierarchy of "epics" and "features" can vary depending on the Agile framework or toolset you're using. In many setups, an *epic* is a large body of work broken down into multiple *features*, while smaller work items (like *user stories*) are nested under those features. However, some tools—such as Atlassian Jira—may not include "features" by default or may structure them differently. The key is to adopt a consistent hierarchy that aligns with your team's workflow and goals.

User Stories

A user story is written from the perspective of the end user and describes a specific interaction or requirement. It follows the format:

"As a [user], I want [action] so that [benefit]."

For example:

- **User Story:** "As a customer, I want to see available time slots so that I can book an appointment easily."

What Does That Mean?

User Stories: Small, user-focused increments of work that describe a specific requirement from the end user's perspective.

Tasks & Sub-Tasks

Tasks are the actionable steps needed to complete a user story. In some cases, tasks can be further divided into sub-tasks if they involve multiple steps or different skill sets (e.g., design vs. backend development).

For example:

- **Task:** Display available time slots in the UI.
    - **Sub-task 1:** Design the slot selection component.
    - **Sub-task 2:** Implement front-end functionality.
    - **Sub-task 3:** Connect to back-end API for real-time availability.

What Does That Mean?

Tasks: Actionable steps required to complete a user story, often broken down into technical or design work.

Note

Some teams treat *tasks* as standalone work items rather than tying them directly to a user story, and instead link *sub-tasks* to user stories. There's no single "right" approach—choose the structure that best fits your team's workflow.

How Agile Requirements Evolve into a Work Breakdown

Agile teams don't start with a fully detailed plan. Instead, they collaborate, refine, and iterate to turn high-level business needs into actionable work items. This process ensures that the team stays aligned with business goals while remaining flexible enough to adapt to change.

This section explains how Agile requirements flow from big-picture ideas to detailed tasks.

1. Understanding Business Needs

Every Agile project starts with a business need—a problem to solve, a market demand, or a customer request. These needs come from stakeholders, leadership, or direct user feedback.

At this stage, the Product Owner (PO) or Product Manager (PM) plays a crucial role in translating business goals into product requirements. They work with stakeholders to answer key questions:

- **What** are we trying to achieve?
- **Who** are we building this for?
- **How** will we measure success?

These discussions shape the Vision & Goals for the product or project, setting the foundation for everything that follows.

What Does That Mean?

Product Owner: The person responsible for defining, prioritizing, and refining work to ensure the team delivers the most valuable product possible. Acting as the custodian of the product vision and roadmap, they bridge the gap between business goals, customer needs, and the development team.

2. *Defining High-Level Requirements*

Once the vision is clear, the Product Owner defines epics—large, high-level requirements that represent significant user needs or business capabilities.

Using the previous example, let's imagine that a company wants to improve its online booking system to reduce frustration and increase customer satisfaction.

- **Vision:** Improve customer satisfaction with our online booking system.
    - **Goal:** Reduce booking time from 5 minutes to under 2 minutes.
        - **Epic:** Allow users to book appointments online.

Epics are too big to complete in a single sprint, so they need to be broken down further. That's where features and user stories come in.

3. Writing User Stories

Agile teams aim to deliver value frequently and in small increments. That's why large items (epics) are broken down into user stories, each focusing on a specific user need or action required to move the epic closer to completion.

A common format is:

"As a [user], I want [action] so that [benefit]."

For example:

- **Feature:** Enable users to select available time slots.
  - **User Story:** "As a customer, I want to see available time slots so that I can book an appointment easily."

User stories are stored in the Product Backlog, where they are continuously reviewed and refined.

4. Refining and Breaking Down Work

Before a user story is ready for development, it needs to be clear, well-defined, and actionable. This happens in Backlog Refinement sessions, where the Agile team:

- Asks clarifying questions.
- Splits large user stories into smaller, more manageable ones.
- Adds Acceptance Criteria to define when a story is complete.
- Identifies technical requirements and risks.

For example:

- **User Story:** "As a customer, I want to see available time slots so that I can book an appointment easily."
    - **Task 1:** Fetch available time slots from the database.
    - **Task 2:** Display available slots in the UI.
    - **Task 3:** Enable selection and confirmation.

For complex tasks, teams might go a step further and create sub-tasks.

This process ensures that when development begins, the work is already well-defined and ready to be executed.

5. Sprint Planning

Once the backlog is refined, the Agile team selects user stories for the upcoming sprint during Sprint Planning. The team decides who will work on what and discusses the best way to implement each task.

A key principle here is Definition of Ready (DoR)—only stories that are clear, properly estimated, and achievable within a sprint are pulled into development.

6. Deliver, Learn, and Improve

At the end of the sprint, the team delivers a working product increment and gathers feedback from stakeholders. Two core events occur here:

- **Sprint Review:** Stakeholders see a demo of the new product features or improvements, provide feedback, and discuss what should come next.
- **Sprint Retrospective:** The team looks at what went well, what didn't, and how they can improve for the next sprint—whether that's about their process, communication, or tools.

Following these events, the Product Owner and the rest of the team reorders the backlog, and the process repeats. This iterative cycle ensures that teams continuously improve both their process and the product.

Acceptance Criteria

Agile thrives on collaboration and adaptability, but without clear guidelines, work can easily become ambiguous. That's where Acceptance Criteria (AC) come in.

They act as a contract between the Product Owner and the development team, ensuring that everyone understands what "done" really means for a user story.

Acceptance criteria are specific conditions that must be met for a user story to be considered complete and acceptable. They define:

- What functionality should work
- How the feature should behave
- Any constraints or expected conditions

Acceptance criteria are typically written in one of two ways: scenario-based (Given-When-Then format) or checklist style. Both approaches help define what needs to be met for a feature to be considered complete.

Acceptance criteria ensure that Agile teams deliver the right functionality, the right way, the first time.

Good acceptance criteria are:

- **Clear:** Free from ambiguity and open to only one interpretation.
- **Testable:** Can be verified through functional or automated testing.
- **Concise:** Focused on what matters, avoiding unnecessary detail.
- **User-focused:** Written from the perspective of how the feature should work for the end user.

Scenario-Based Acceptance Criteria (Given-When-Then Format)

This format, inspired by Behavior-Driven Development (BDD), describes the system behavior in specific scenarios.

User Story:

"As a customer, I want to reset my password so that I can regain access to my account."

Acceptance Criteria:

- **Given** I am on the login page, **when** I click "Forgot Password," **then** I should be redirected to the password reset page.
- **Given** I enter an unregistered email, **when** I request a reset link, **then** I should see an error message.
- **Given** I enter my registered email, **when** I request a reset link, **then** I should receive a reset email.

This structure makes it easy to test and verify behavior.

Checklist Format (Simple Bullet Points)

Sometimes, a straightforward checklist-style format is preferred, especially for UI-related requirements.

User Story:

"As a user, I want to see available time slots so that I can book an appointment easily."

Acceptance Criteria:

- The system displays only available time slots.
- Users can select a time slot and confirm their selection.
- A confirmation message is displayed after booking.
- Users cannot select a time slot in the past.

This approach works well for simpler stories that don't require multiple conditions or user flows.

Definition of Ready

In Agile, a common challenge teams face is starting work too soon—before requirements are clear, dependencies are resolved, or acceptance criteria are properly defined. This often leads to delays, rework, and misaligned expectations. The Definition of Ready (DoR) prevents this by setting clear entry criteria for work to be considered ready for development.

> Sprint planning works best when the backlog is well-refined and ready to go. The DoR streamlines this process by ensuring that:
>
> - Teams don't waste time discussing vague or incomplete work.
> - Developers can estimate effort more accurately, leading to better sprint commitments.
> - Stories flow smoothly through the sprint with fewer blockers.
>
> When every work item meets the Definition of Ready, teams can focus on building and delivering value, rather than scrambling to clarify requirements mid-sprint.

How the Definition of Ready Works

The DoR acts as a quality filter before a user story enters a sprint. If a story doesn't meet the criteria, it's either refined further or deprioritized until it's truly ready.

Common Definition of Ready criteria:

- The story is clearly defined and follows the user story format *(As a [user], I want [feature] so that [benefit]).*
- Acceptance criteria are written and agreed upon.
- Dependencies (technical, legal, or business) are identified and resolved.
- The story is small enough to be completed within a sprint.
- The team understands the scope and has no open questions.

If a story does not meet these conditions, it goes back into Backlog Refinement for further clarification.

Definition of Done

In Agile, work isn't just "done" when a developer writes the last line of code, or a designer finalizes an interface. It's only truly done when it meets all the necessary quality standards, is fully tested, and is ready for deployment.

That's where the Definition of Done (DoD) comes in. The DoD is a shared agreement within the Agile team that sets clear criteria for when a task, user story, or product increment is considered fully complete.

The Definition of Done is more than a checklist—it's a quality gate that keeps Agile teams focused on delivering high-quality, fully completed work. By aligning everyone on what "done" really means, teams avoid unfinished work, last-minute surprises, and inconsistent delivery.

A good DoD should be:

- **Clear:** No ambiguity on what "done" means.
- **Measurable:** Each criterion should be verifiable.
- **Agreed upon:** The entire Agile team (developers, testers, Product Owner) should align on it.

How Definition of Done Works

The DoD applies at multiple levels, ensuring that all work meets the necessary standards before moving forward.

Table 7: Definition of Done (DoD)

Level	Definition of Done
User Story	• Code is written, peer-reviewed, and merged into the main branch. • Unit tests and integration tests have passed. • The feature works on supported devices and browsers. • The story meets its Acceptance Criteria. • UI and functionality have been verified by QA. Product Owner has reviewed and approved it.
Sprint	• Fully tested and reviewed. • Integrated into the main codebase. • Ready to be deployed, if necessary.
Release	• All planned user stories meet the DoD. • Regression testing has been completed. • The release package is fully deployable with no outstanding defects. • Documentation is updated (release notes, user guides, etc.). • Deployment has been approved by relevant stakeholders.

Definition of Done vs. Acceptance Criteria

A common point of confusion is the difference between Acceptance Criteria and the Definition of Done. While they are related, they serve different purposes.

Table 8: Definition of Done vs. Acceptance Criteria

Aspect	Acceptance Criteria	Definition of Done
Scope	Specific to a single user story.	Applies across all work items.
Purpose	Defines when a specific feature meets requirements.	Defines when any work item is truly complete.
Example	"A user can reset their password via email."	"All code is peer-reviewed and tested before deployment."

Velocity

Agile teams thrive on iteration and continuous delivery, but they also need a way to track how much work they're completing and how to plan future sprints realistically. That's where velocity comes in.

Velocity is a measurement of the amount of work a team completes in a sprint, typically measured in story points, tasks, or other effort-based units. It helps teams understand their delivery capacity so they can forecast future work more accurately.

> One of the biggest misconceptions about velocity is that it should be used to measure team performance—but this is not its purpose.
>
> Velocity shouldn't be used to compare teams. Different teams estimate velocity differently, making it meaningless for comparison.
>
> Velocity shouldn't be used to pressure teams into "increasing output." The goal is not to maximize velocity but to ensure stable, predictable delivery.
>
> Velocity is a tool for teams, not a performance scoreboard. It helps teams understand their capacity so they can commit to a sustainable amount of work per sprint.

How Teams Use Velocity for Planning and Forecasting

Velocity is calculated by tracking the total number of completed story points (or work items) per sprint. Over several sprints, the team's average velocity becomes a useful planning tool.

For example:

- **Sprint 1:** The team completes 20 story points.
- **Sprint 2:** The team completes 22 story points.
- **Sprint 3:** The team completes 18 story points.
- **Average Velocity:** 20 story points per sprint.

If a team's average velocity is 20 story points per sprint, they can use this to forecast how much work they can take on in future sprints.

If a project backlog contains 100 story points of work, and the team's velocity is 20 points per sprint, they can estimate that the project will take five sprints to complete (assuming stable conditions).

What Does That Mean?

Story points: Story points are a relative measure used in Agile to estimate the effort required to complete a task or user story. They consider complexity, effort, and risk, rather than specific time estimates.

Backlog Refinement

Backlog refinement is the process of reviewing, updating, and prioritizing items in the product backlog to ensure they are clear, properly scoped, and ready for development. It prevents last-minute surprises by ensuring that the highest-priority work is well-defined before sprint planning.

> A well-maintained backlog is the backbone of an efficient Agile team. Without regular refinement, the backlog can become cluttered, unclear, or misaligned with business priorities, leading to confusion and delays.
>
> A cluttered, poorly maintained backlog can create serious problems:
>
> - **Vague or incomplete stories** lead to wasted time clarifying requirements mid-sprint.
> - **Overloaded backlogs** make it hard to prioritize what really matters.
> - **Lack of refinement** leads to last-minute scrambling, causing stress and inefficiency.

Best Practices for Backlog Refinement

1. Make It a Regular Practice

Backlog refinement should happen continuously, with dedicated sessions before sprint planning to review and update backlog items.

2. Prioritize What Matters

Focus on high-value items first. Use prioritization techniques like MoSCoW (Must-have, Should-have, Could-have, Won't-have) or Weighted Shortest Job First (WSJF) to ensure effort is spent on what delivers the most impact.

3. Break Down Large Stories

Big stories (epics) should be split into smaller, testable, and independently deliverable user stories to avoid delays.

4. Ensure Stories Meet the Definition of Ready (DoR)

A story should not enter a sprint unless it is fully defined and actionable. Ask:

- Is the user story clear and formatted properly?
- Does it have Acceptance Criteria?
- Are dependencies resolved?
- Can it be completed within a sprint?

5. Keep the Backlog Lean

Remove outdated, low-priority, or unnecessary items to keep the backlog focused and actionable.

5

Scrum

Introduction

Scrum is one of the most widely used Agile frameworks, designed to help teams deliver value quickly, adapt to change, and continuously improve. It provides a structured yet flexible framework for managing work in complex environments, establishing a scaffolding of roles, events, and artifacts that enable Agile teams to build great products—again and again.

Unlike traditional project management methods that rely on rigid, upfront planning, Scrum embraces flexibility and iteration. It empowers teams to respond to changing requirements, prioritize work dynamically, and deliver working solutions incrementally. This makes Scrum particularly effective in fast-paced environments where customer needs evolve rapidly.

In this chapter, we'll explore how Scrum puts Agile principles into action. You'll learn how Scrum teams are structured, how work is organized, and how key events keep teams aligned and continuously improving. By the end, you'll have a clear understanding of how Scrum enables teams to stay adaptable, collaborate effectively, and consistently deliver high-quality products—all while staying true to Agile values.

What Is Scrum?

Scrum is the most popular Agile framework—think of it as a structured way to put Agile's values and principles into daily practice. While Agile defines *what* matters—collaboration, customer feedback, and responding to change—Scrum lays out *how* to do it, giving teams a clear blueprint for turning lofty ideals into tangible action. Despite its structured approach, Scrum still leaves enough room for creativity to thrive, offering repeatable processes that spark ongoing innovation.

Although originally created for software development, Scrum has been adopted in many other domains, from process improvements to marketing campaigns (Quick 2024). Its disciplined yet flexible nature empowers teams to organize their work in short, focused cycles called sprints. Within these timeboxed periods, the team plans, builds, inspects, and adapts together—ensuring they can quickly pivot if requirements shift, or new ideas emerge. This blend of structure and adaptability is exactly why Scrum remains the world's most popular Agile framework today.

:

Scrum Workflow

Compared to traditional, sequential methods where change is often viewed as an unwelcome detour, Scrum is built on the idea that change can (and should) happen along the way. By following a cyclical, iterative routine, Scrum creates constant opportunities to gather feedback, incorporate new insights, and adapt accordingly.

At each stage of the workflow, stakeholders and team members collaborate to refine the product, ensuring it meets real needs rather than just ticking off predetermined requirements. Through regular communication—daily check-ins, Sprint Reviews, and Retrospectives—the Scrum team learns what works, identifies what doesn't, and pivots as needed. This consistent loop of inspect-and-adapt is what makes Scrum so powerful. Instead of viewing unforeseen changes as failures in planning, teams see them as chances for innovation and growth.

Refer to Figure 17 below to see how these Scrum events flow in a continuous cycle. As the team refines its approach with each sprint, efficiency and productivity tend to climb. Over time, this iterative process builds a rhythm of constant improvement—one that's agile enough to welcome new ideas and shifting priorities without derailing the entire project.

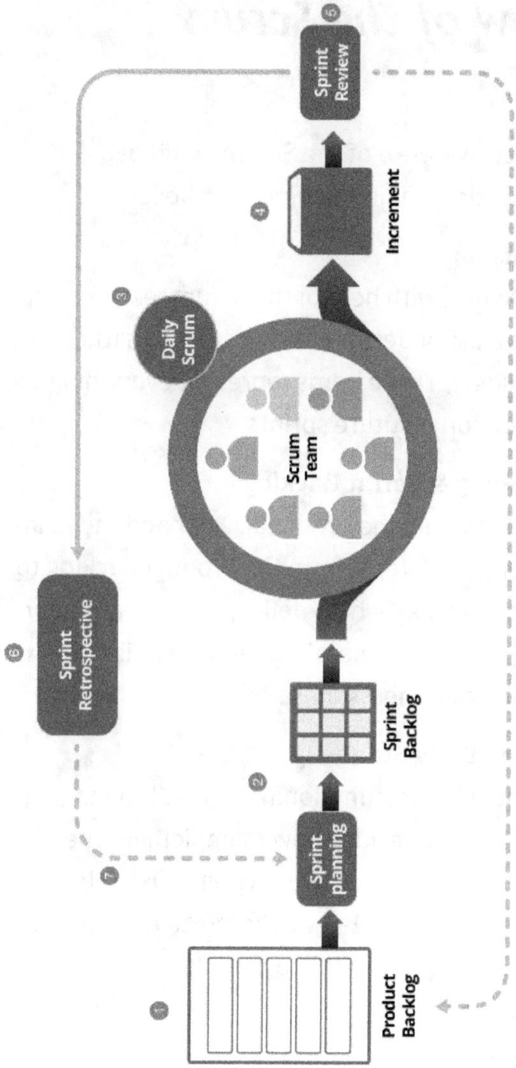

Figure 17: Stages in the Scrum Workflow

Overview of the Scrum Workflow

Here's a concise overview of the Scrum workflow, explaining each element in the diagram above:

1. Product Backlog
The Product Owner, with help of the Scrum team, creates and prioritizes a list of desired features or tasks (the "Product Backlog"). These items represent everything the team might work on in future sprints.

2. Sprint Planning & Sprint Backlog
During Sprint Planning, the Product Owner and the team select the top-priority items from the Product Backlog to form the Sprint Backlog, which defines specific goals for the upcoming sprint. The team's commitment is to deliver working product that meets these goals.

3. Daily Scrum / Daily Stand-Up
The Development Team, functioning as a self-managing, cross-functional unit, decides how to implement the selected backlog items. They work within a fixed timebox called a sprint (commonly 1–4 weeks). Each day, they hold a short daily meeting (often called the "Daily Scrum" or "Daily Stand-Up") to synchronize efforts and quickly address any issues.

The Scrum Master facilitates the process, ensuring the team remains focused on its sprint goals and removing any obstacles that might slow their progress.

4. Potentially Shippable Increment

By the end of the sprint, the team aims to produce a "potentially shippable increment"—an updated version of the product that meets the team's definition of "done." This increment is usually composed of finished Product Backlog Items (PBIs) and user stories and is ready for demonstration or even release to stakeholders..

5. Sprint Review

The second-to-last event of the sprint is the Sprint Review, where the team showcases completed work to stakeholders and gathers feedback. This feedback can influence the Product Backlog and planning for upcoming sprints.

6. Sprint Retrospective

The final event of the sprint is a retrospective meeting held exclusively among the Scrum Team to reflect on their processes, celebrating what went well and identifying areas for improvement.

7. Repeat

With the sprint complete, the team selects the next set of high-priority items from the Product Backlog, forming a new Sprint Backlog to begin the next sprint cycle. The cycle then begins again with Sprint Planning—see **Step 2.**

Visualizing the Work

To keep track of what's happening, Scrum teams rely on "information radiators"—visible tools like task boards and burndown charts. These make it easy for both the team and stakeholders to see what's in progress, what's done, and what still needs attention.

What Does That Mean?

Information Radiators: Visual displays (e.g., a task board on the wall, an online Kanban board, or a sprint burndown chart) that broadcast the team's status at a glance. By "radiating" information outward, these tools allow everyone—team members, Scrum Master, Product Owner, and stakeholders—to understand the current state of development, discuss bottlenecks, and make quick decisions whenever needed.

Scrum Roles

One of the reasons Scrum works so well is its balance between a straightforward process and clearly defined roles. Each role has its own responsibilities, but they all work in sync to keep the team moving forward—without burying anyone under layers of complex rules. At the heart of this deceptively simple system are three key roles: Product Owner, Scrum Master, and Development Team.

Product Owner

The Product Owner is accountable for defining, prioritizing, and refining work to ensure the team delivers the most valuable product possible. Acting as the custodian of the product vision and roadmap, they bridge the gap between business goals, customer needs, and the development team.

Their primary role is to manage the Product Backlog, ensuring it remains well-defined, prioritized, and aligned with strategic objectives. They decide which features, enhancements, or fixes are most important—often tracking these items in tools like Atlassian's Jira or Azure DevOps—and continuously reorder the backlog based on new insights, market changes, and stakeholder feedback.

The Product Owner collaborates with the team to select which backlog items will be worked on next, ensuring that work progresses in the right direction and aligns with evolving priorities. By breaking down high-level business objectives into epics, features, and user stories, they help create clear, actionable requirements that guide the team's efforts.

Table 9: Key Responsibilities of the Product Owner

Responsibility	Refined Description
Formulate & Uphold Product Vision	Define and refine the product vision to align with business strategy, market conditions, and user needs.
Represent the Business	Act as the link between the Scrum team and stakeholders, ensuring the product aligns with business goals and customer needs.
Engage with Customers	Gather and incorporate customer feedback, usage data, and market research into backlog decisions.
Provide Business Expertise	Offer insights, industry knowledge, and business context to help the team understand feature priorities.
Prioritize Backlog Items	Own the Product Backlog, ranking features and fixes to deliver the most value to users and the organization.
Continuously Refine the Backlog	Keep the backlog structured and prioritized, adjusting based on new insights, shifting priorities, and feedback.
Collaborate with the Scrum Master & Dev. Team	Work with the Scrum Master and Development Team to optimize Agile processes, remove blockers, and enhance team performance.
Manage Revenue and Costs	Balance product investment and sustainability, ensuring features align with budget constraints and business goals.

Scrum Master

The Scrum Master is a servant-leader who coaches, facilitates, and enables teams to apply Scrum effectively. Unlike a traditional manager or project lead, the Scrum Master does not "manage" the Development Team. Instead, they focus on helping teams self-organize, improving Agile adoption, and removing obstacles that hinder progress.

Beyond the team, the Scrum Master also supports the wider organization in embracing Scrum, ensuring smooth collaboration, and fostering a culture of continuous improvement. By removing impediments and facilitating communication, they help teams focus on delivering value efficiently and sustainably.

What Does That Mean?

Servant Leadership: A leadership approach where the leader's primary role is to support, empower, and enable their team rather than command or control. A servant leader prioritizes the growth, well-being, and success of the team, removes obstacles, and fosters a culture of trust, collaboration, and continuous improvement.

Table 10: Key Responsibilities of the Scrum Master

Responsibility	Description
Coach the Team & Organization	Guide team members, stakeholders, and leadership in understanding and embracing Scrum values, principles, and practices.
Facilitate Scrum Events	Ensure effective execution of Scrum events, including Sprint Planning, Daily Stand-Ups, Sprint Reviews, and Retrospectives.
Manage Impediments	Identify and mitigate obstacles that hinder the team's progress, whether technical, administrative, or organizational.
Promote Collaboration	Cultivate an open, trusting environment where team members can share ideas, provide feedback, and resolve conflicts smoothly.
Shield the Team	Protect the team from external distractions or demands that aren't sprint priorities, ensuring they can stay on task.
Foster Continuous Improvement	Encourage a culture of regular review and adaptation, allowing the team to refine processes, enhance collaboration, and improve overall performance.

Development Team

The Development Team is a self-managing, cross-functional group of specialists—such as developers, designers, and testers—who work together to achieve the sprint goal. They plan, estimate, and build the backlog items prioritized by the Product Owner, ensuring that each product increment meets the Definition of Done and is potentially shippable by the end of the sprint.

With the freedom to decide how much work they can take on and how to complete it, the Development Team plays a crucial role in bringing Agile principles to life. By combining their different skills and expertise, they take full ownership of how work is completed and delivered, ensuring high-quality outcomes with every sprint.

Table 11: Key Responsibilities of the Development Team

Responsibility	Description
Self-Manage	Determine how much work can be realistically completed in a sprint and choose the most efficient way to accomplish it.
Collaborate Cross-Functionally	Work together across development, design, and testing to solve problems and build high-quality features.
Own the Sprint Backlog	Maintain and update the Sprint Backlog, track progress, and ensure transparency in achieving the sprint goal.
Deliver Product Increments	Plan, develop, test, and finalize prioritized features to produce a potentially shippable product increment each sprint.
Adapt & Improve	Incorporate feedback from Sprint Reviews and Retrospectives to continuously refine both the product and team processes.

Scrum Artifacts

Scrum artifacts capture the key information and outputs that make work visible and enable collaboration, inspection, and adaptation. Think of them as the "what" of the Scrum process—where all the team's iterative work comes together in a transparent, inspectable form.

If you're familiar with traditional project management, Scrum artifacts—such as the Product Backlog, Sprint Backlog, and Increment—may seem similar to project plans, schedules, or scope documents. However, unlike waterfall approaches, Scrum artifacts are continuously refined throughout the sprint, allowing teams to adjust priorities, incorporate new insights, and respond to evolving requirements in real time.

These artifacts provide a simple yet powerful system for managing work in small, iterative chunks. Because backlog items can be reordered and reprioritized every sprint, Scrum ensures that teams always focus on the most valuable work at any given time.

Most importantly, Scrum artifacts promote transparency and alignment by giving developers, Product Owners, and stakeholders a clear, real-time view of work in progress. This visibility ensures that teams can track progress, stay aligned, and quickly adapt as circumstances change.

Product Backlog

[illegible]

Product Backlog

At the heart of Scrum is the Product Backlog: an ordered list of epics, features, user stories, and bug fixes—everything needed to deliver a successful product. By prioritizing backlog items based on business value, user needs, and strategic objectives, the team ensures each sprint tackles the most important tasks first.

Importantly, the backlog is not fixed. Using a "just in time" approach to planning, the Product Owner continually refines and reprioritizes this list, incorporating new insights, feedback, and market changes.

This constant revision means the team always has a fresh, relevant set of items to pull into the Sprint Backlog. Over time, the Product Owner may add more detail, remove outdated tasks, or reshuffle priorities, keeping everyone aligned on what truly matters and why.

Priority	User Story
1	As a customer, I want to see available time slots so I can book an appointment easily.
2	As a customer, I want to receive a confirmation email after booking to ensure my appointment is scheduled.
3	As a customer, I want to cancel or reschedule my appointment so I can manage my bookings flexibly.
4	As a customer, I want to pay for my booking securely so I can confirm my appointment instantly.
5	As a customer, I want to choose from multiple payment methods so I can use my preferred option.
6	As a business owner, I want to view and manage upcoming appointments so I can allocate resources effectively.
7	As a customer, I want to receive a reminder notification before my appointment so I don't miss it.

Figure 18: Example Product Backlog

Sprint Backlog

The Sprint Backlog is a subset of the Product Backlog that the Development Team selects during Sprint Planning to complete within a single sprint. It contains user stories, tasks, and defects that contribute to achieving the Sprint Goal—a guiding objective that defines the sprint's purpose.

Think of the Sprint Backlog as the team's short-term action plan—a structured list of work that is realistic, achievable, and timeboxed. By focusing on a manageable scope, the team ensures steady progress without becoming overwhelmed.

What Does That Mean?

Sprint Goal: A concise statement that describes the intended outcome of the sprint. It provides direction and focus, helping the team align their efforts while allowing flexibility in how they achieve it.

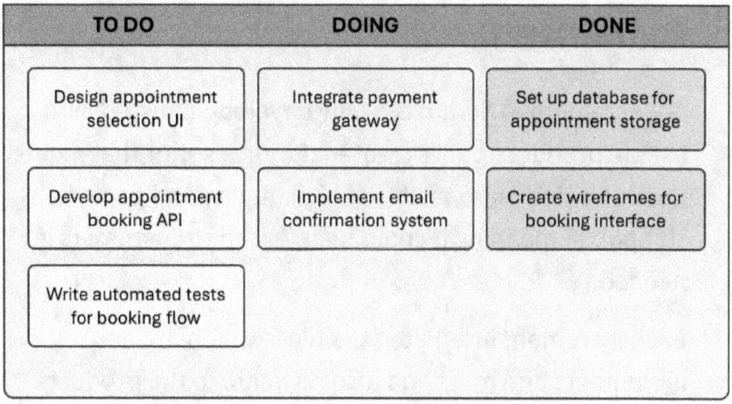

Figure 19: Example Sprint Board

Increment

An Increment in Scrum is a fully developed, tested, and usable product update created during a sprint that meets the Definition of Done. It is of high quality and potentially shippable, meaning it could be released to customers if needed.

Each increment integrates seamlessly with previous increments and must add distinct value to the product. While Scrum does not require every increment to be immediately shipped, it ensures that teams consistently produce work that is in a releasable state.

By maintaining a potentially shippable increment at the end of every sprint, teams can release updates frequently, gather user feedback, and make continuous improvements.

Difference between Increment and PBI:

- **Increment**: The result of completing one or more PBIs during a sprint. It is a tangible, usable, and potentially shippable product update that meets the Definition of Done.
- **Product Backlog Item (PBI)**: An individual item on the Product Backlog that represents a task, feature, bug fix, or requirement that needs to be completed. PBIs are the building blocks of an Increment and are prioritized and selected during Sprint Planning.

Table 12: Example Increment

Completed User Stories	Potentially Shippable?	Value Added
As a customer, I want to see available time slots so I can book an appointment easily.	Yes	Customers can now view available time slots.
As a customer, I want to receive a confirmation email after booking to ensure my appointment is scheduled.	Yes	Customers receive confirmation emails for booked appointments.
As a customer, I want to cancel or reschedule my appointment so I can manage my bookings flexibly.	Yes	Customers can manage, reschedule, or cancel their bookings online.

Scrum Events

Scrum runs on a structured rhythm of events that keep the team focused, aligned, and continuously improving. These events aren't just meetings—they're purposeful feedback loops designed to help teams plan, track progress, and adapt as needed. Each event is timeboxed, ensuring efficiency while maintaining enough structure for meaningful feedback and collaboration.

Scrum events create a predictable workflow that keeps things moving smoothly. From planning the sprint to daily check-ins, each event plays a crucial role in helping teams work iteratively and deliver value consistently.

Insight: Why Scrum Events Matter

Scrum events aren't just routine meetings—they are outcome-driven sessions designed to replace unnecessary meetings and keep teams focused on delivering value. Each event has a clear purpose and is meant to drive progress, gather feedback, alignment, and improvement rather than disrupt work.

In short, Scrum events exist to keep teams productive, engaged, and continuously improving—not to add more meetings to their calendar.

The core Scrum events include:

- **Sprint Planning:** Deciding what work the team will take on for the sprint.
- **Daily Scrum (Stand-ups):** A quick, daily check-in to sync up on progress and roadblocks.
- **Backlog Refinement:** Regularly updating and prioritizing the Product Backlog.
- **Sprint Review:** Showcasing completed work and gathering feedback.
- **Sprint Retrospective:** Reflecting on what went well, what didn't, and how to improve for next time.

Together, these events create the heartbeat of Scrum, helping teams stay on track, collaborate effectively, and make continuous improvements—one sprint at a time.

Sprint Planning

Sprint Planning kicks off each sprint, bringing the Scrum Team and Product Owner together to decide what work will be completed in the upcoming sprint. This timeboxed meeting ensures that the team has clarity, alignment, and a shared focus before development begins.

During Sprint Planning, the team:

- **Reviews the Product Backlog:** Looking at the highest-priority user stories and backlog items.
- **Defines the Sprint Goal:** A clear, guiding objective for the sprint.
- **Selects backlog items to work on:** Choosing a realistic workload based on team capacity.

The sprint officially begins once planning is complete, with the team focusing on the agreed-upon user stories and tasks throughout the sprint. By aligning early, teams avoid confusion, work efficiently, and stay focused on delivering meaningful value by the sprint's end.

Insight: Typical Timebox for Sprint Planning

The typical timebox for Sprint Planning depends on the length of the sprint:

1-week sprint → 2 hours

2-week sprint → 4 hours

3-week sprint → 6 hours

4-week sprint → 8 hours (maximum)

The *Scrum Guide* (Schwaber and Sutherland 2020) recommends up to 8 hours for a one-month sprint, with shorter sprints having proportionally shorter planning meetings. The goal is to keep it efficient while ensuring clarity on what needs to be done.

Daily Scrum

The Daily Scrum (or stand-up) is a 15-minute timeboxed meeting where the Development Team syncs up, surfaces blockers, and plans the next 24 hours of work. This quick check-in helps the team stay aligned and ensures steady progress toward the Sprint Goal.

During the Daily Scrum, team members typically answer three key questions:

1. What did I do yesterday to achieve the Sprint Goal?
2. What will I work on today to achieve the Sprint Goal?
3. Are there any blockers preventing progress?

Held at the same time and place every day, the Daily Scrum keeps the team focused and responsive to challenges. Unlike traditional status meetings, it is not led by a manager or Scrum Master—the Development Team runs the meeting themselves, reinforcing self-management.

While standing up is a common practice to keep the meeting short, it's not a requirement—what matters is keeping discussions concise, relevant, and action-driven.

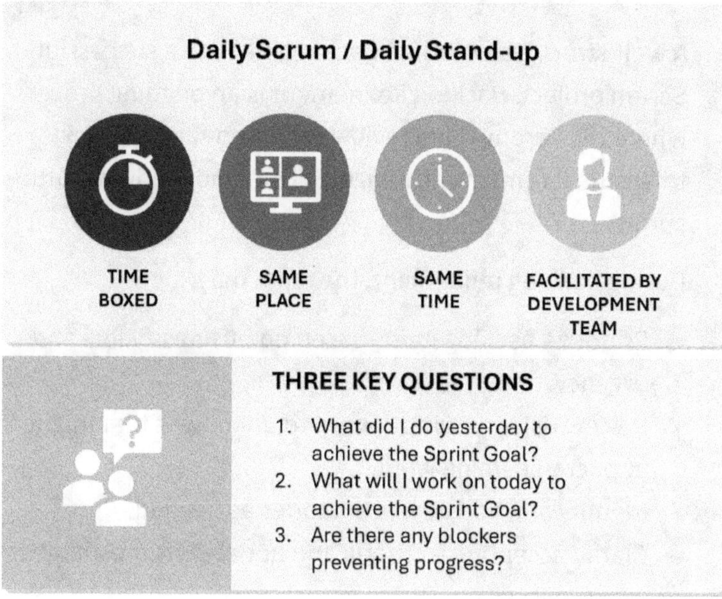

Figure 20: Daily Scrum / Daily Stand-up

Backlog Refinement

A well-structured Product Backlog is key to a successful Scrum project. Backlog Refinement is an ongoing process where the Scrum Team reviews and updates the backlog to ensure it remains prioritized, clear, and ready for future sprints.

During backlog refinement, the team may:

- Prioritize backlog items based on business value and urgency.
- Review risks, assumptions, and unknowns that might impact upcoming work.
- Identify and add new user stories as needed.
- Clarify acceptance criteria and update effort estimates where necessary.
- Break down large user stories into smaller, more manageable pieces.

Note

Backlog Refinement is not an official Scrum event, but it is a recommended practice. It can be done as a scheduled session or whenever needed throughout the sprint. Many teams find that holding a refinement session midway through the sprint helps them stay aligned and prepare for Sprint Planning.

Sprint Reviews

The Sprint Review takes place on the last day of the sprint and serves as an opportunity for the Scrum Team to demonstrate their completed work to stakeholders and gather feedback. This informal, interactive session allows the team to showcase progress, validate assumptions, and discuss next steps based on stakeholder input.

Unlike a simple demo, the Sprint Review is a collaborative discussion where stakeholders provide feedback that may influence future backlog priorities. The Product Owner takes note of insights to help refine the backlog and ensure that upcoming work continues to align with business needs.

Key features of the Sprint Review:

- Occurs at the end of the sprint.
- The Scrum Team presents their completed work to stakeholders.
- Stakeholder feedback is gathered to refine the Product Backlog and inform future Sprint Planning.

Beyond being a functional checkpoint, Sprint Reviews boost morale by giving the team a chance to appreciate their work in a supportive environment while ensuring that what's being built continues to deliver value.:

Sprint Retrospective

Following the Sprint Review, the Scrum Team holds a Sprint Retrospective, a team-only session dedicated to reflection, learning, and continuous improvement. This is the team's chance to discuss:

- What went well?
- What didn't go well?
- What can be improved in the next sprint?

The Sprint Retrospective is private, meaning only the Scrum Team attends. This allows for open, honest discussions about process improvements without external pressure.

Unlike the Sprint Review, which focuses on the product, the Sprint Retrospective focuses on the team's way of working. This is where the team evaluates unfinished Sprint Backlog items, workflow challenges, collaboration issues, or tooling concerns, and agrees on concrete actions for improvement.

6

The Agile Mindset

Introduction

The Agile mindset is more than just following an Agile framework like Scrum or Kanban—it's about thinking and working in a way that reflects Agile values and principles. It shapes how teams approach problems, collaboration, and change, guiding them toward flexibility, continuous improvement, and delivering value.

This mindset originates from the *Agile Manifesto's* four values and twelve principles, which prioritize:

- Individuals and interactions over processes and tools.
- Working software over comprehensive documentation.
- Customer collaboration over contract negotiation.
- Responding to change over following a plan.

While Agile frameworks provide structure, it's the Agile mindset that makes them effective. Without it, teams risk treating Agile like a checklist rather than embracing the adaptive, people-centric philosophy that makes it work.

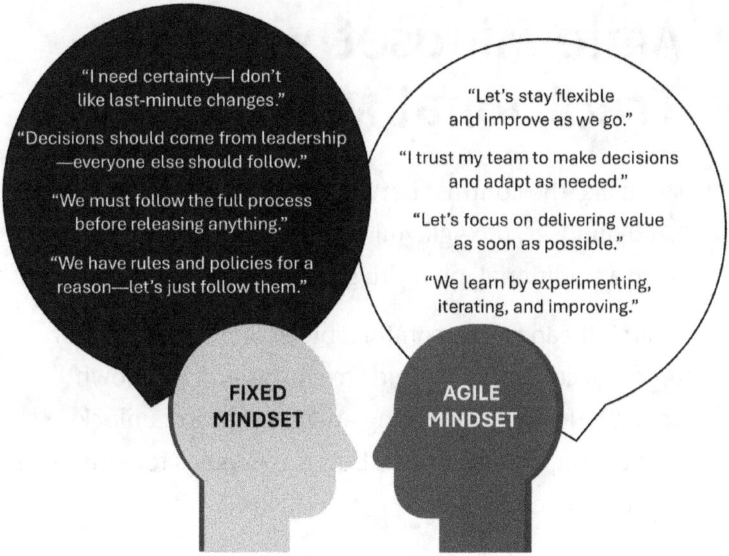

Figure 21: Traditional Mindset vs. Agile Mindset

Agile Mindset vs. Traditional Mindset

Much like the contrast between a growth mindset and a fixed mindset, the Agile mindset differs fundamentally from a traditional, plan-driven mindset.

This shift can feel uncomfortable at first, especially for teams accustomed to rigid structures and top-down control. However, adopting an Agile mindset unlocks innovation, efficiency, and better outcomes for both teams and customers.

Table 13: Agile and Traditional (Fixed) Mindsets Compared

Agile Mindset	Traditional (Fixed) Mindset
Values flexibility and continuous improvement	Values certainty and rigid planning
Embraces change as a way to improve the product	Sees change as a disruption to the plan
Trusts teams to self-manage and adapt	Relies on top-down decision-making
Encourages learning, experimentation, and iteration	Follows strict policies, processes, and rules

Servant Leadership

In Agile, leadership isn't about giving orders—it's about removing roadblocks, fostering collaboration, and enabling teams to succeed. This approach is known as servant leadership, where the leader's primary role is to support the team, not control it.

A servant leader focuses on:

- **Empowering the team:** Trusting them to make decisions and self-organize.
- **Removing obstacles:** Helping clear roadblocks that slow down progress.
- **Facilitating collaboration:** Encouraging open communication and alignment.
- **Driving continuous improvement:** Helping the team reflect, learn, and adapt.

Unlike traditional command-and-control leadership, where decisions flow from the top down, servant leaders listen first, coach rather than dictate, and create an environment where people feel safe to take ownership.

How to apply servant leadership:

- **Ask, "How can I help?"** Instead of directing work, focus on supporting the team's needs.
- **Give the team autonomy:** Provide clear goals, but let the team decide how to achieve them.
- **Shield the team from distractions:** Protect their focus and time by managing external pressures.
- **Facilitate problem-solving:** Help the team remove blockers, not just work around them.

A true servant leader measures success not by personal achievements, but by how well their team thrives.

What Does That Mean?

Servant Leadership: A leadership approach where the leader's primary role is to support, empower, and enable their team rather than command or control. A servant leader prioritizes the growth, well-being, and success of the team, removes obstacles, and fosters a culture of trust, collaboration, and continuous improvement.

Shifting from Traditional to Agile Mindset

Picture this: you're accustomed to a rigid, step-by-step waterfall process, and suddenly you're asked to "go Agile"—where priorities can change on a dime, and everyone's expected to collaborate and adapt continuously. It's normal to feel a bit disoriented at first. But with Agile, you gain the freedom to respond to real-time customer feedback, pivot effectively, and deliver more value, faster.

Here are some practical tips to help you and your team make the leap:

1. Take Small Steps

Don't try to overhaul everything at once. Start by introducing one Agile principle—like shorter feedback cycles or more collaborative planning—and see how it works.

2. Prioritize Learning Over Perfection

Agile isn't about getting everything right immediately—it's about continuous learning and iteration. Celebrate progress, learn from mistakes, and keep improving.

3. Deliver Value Quickly

Instead of waiting for everything to be "perfect", focus on delivering something small but valuable early. Quick wins build momentum and trust in Agile ways of working.

4. Build a Culture of Trust

Agile thrives in environments where teams feel safe to speak up, experiment, and make decisions. Encourage openness, honest feedback, and shared responsibility.

5. Be Flexible with Methods

Agile isn't about forcing everyone into Scrum, Kanban, or SAFe—it's about adapting practices to fit your needs while staying true to Agile principles.

When *Isn't* Agile Suitable?

The Agile mindset—putting customers first, working together, staying flexible, and always improving—can work almost anywhere. We're strong believers in this approach! However, not every team or project can easily adopt a formal Agile framework like Scrum, Kanban, or SAFe, each of which relies on short, repeated cycles ("sprints") and regular reordering of priorities.

Construction: Strict Sequences and Long Lead Times

Construction projects typically involve a chain of dependent steps—for example: Dig Foundations → Install Rebar → (and only then) Pour Concrete.

Each activity depends on the previous one being finished properly, and subcontractors often schedule their teams months or even years in advance.

If you suddenly decide, "Let's move pouring concrete to next month instead of next week," it can trigger a chain reaction that disrupts the entire schedule and inflates costs. While Agile principles (like regular check-ins) can be used in early design or planning, the hands-on construction phase usually has far less flexibility.

Consulting: Fixed Deliverables and Contracts

Consultants and contractors often work under detailed contracts with defined deliverables, milestones, and payment schedules—especially when working with government clients, who must follow strict procurement rules. For instance, a consulting firm may be contracted to deliver a strategic plan, broken down into carefully specified phases, each with its own deadline and payment trigger. These fixed milestones can rule out the short, iterative cycles that Agile relies on. Introducing sprints, frequent backlog changes, or other Agile practices often means altering agreed-upon scope or schedules, which can be expensive and time-consuming—something many clients prefer to avoid.

Common Thread: Heavy Dependencies and High Stakes

In these examples, reshuffling tasks mid-project can create major problems. Think of it this way: if you need to reorder tasks and respond to feedback frequently, an Agile framework fits well. But if reordering causes big disruptions, excessive costs, or significant risks, then Agile might not be as effective.

That said, the Agile mindset—open communication, continuous learning, and a strong focus on delivering value—can still be a tremendous asset. Even if you're not running full sprints, strategically applying Agile principles can enhance collaboration and keep you focused on what truly matters.

Continuous Practice: Keeping Your Agile Mindset Sharp

Building an Agile mindset isn't a one-and-done activity—it's something intrinsic that you refine every day with your team. To keep your Agile thinking sharp, focus on your day-to-day interactions and rituals.

Here are a few practical ways to put Agile into practice:

- **Join (or facilitate) Daily Scrums:** Keep updates concise and action-oriented.
- **Actively contribute to Sprint Planning:** Help define clear, achievable sprint goals.
- **Engage in Sprint Reviews:** Gather feedback, adjust priorities, and keep the focus on value.
- **Lead (or participate in) Sprint Retrospectives:** Reflect on ways to improve team collaboration and efficiency.

Our Final Word...

Agile is not just a framework—it's a mindset. While frameworks provide structure and best practices, true agility comes from embracing adaptability, collaboration, and delivering value in a way that fits your team's needs.

Being Agile means understanding that no single framework is one-size-fits-all. Some elements—like short feedback loops, prioritizing the most valuable work, and holding regular retrospectives—can be applied immediately. Others—like shifting from command-and-control leadership to self-managing teams—may take time and practice. The key is to start small, experiment, and refine as you go.

As you progress, Agile will become second nature—not something you simply "do," but something you apply instinctively. You'll move beyond following processes to thinking in Agile terms, constantly asking:

- Are we working on the most valuable thing right now?
- Are we learning from feedback and adjusting accordingly?
- Are we collaborating effectively as a team?

Throughout this book, you've seen that Agile isn't about blindly following rules—it's about delivering value, embracing change, and continuously improving.

To put this into practice, start by making small, meaningful changes in your daily work:

- **Start with small changes**—run a retrospective, break down work into smaller increments, or prioritize backlog refinement.
- **Look for ways to get feedback faster**—from users, stakeholders, or within your team.
- **Encourage open conversations**—foster a culture where challenges are discussed early, and solutions emerge together.
- **Make improvement a habit**—after every sprint, ask: *What's one thing we can do better next time?*

More than just improving processes, an Agile mindset helps create a work environment where creativity thrives, collaboration is seamless, and adaptability becomes a competitive advantage.

So, as you move forward, focus on what works for your team, stay open to learning, and most importantly—deliver value, one iteration at a time.

Unlock More Learning

Read this book online at no cost, explore other Boffin Education titles, and download templates and samples. Simply use the code **AGILE101ULTIMATE** to activate your 12-month free membership in our professional library. Visit Boffin Education online, follow the prompts, and start exploring today!

7

Glossary

Term	Definition
Agile	A project management and product development philosophy that emphasizes iterative progress, adaptability, and continuous value delivery.
Agile Framework	A structured approach that applies Agile principles through defined roles, workflows, and practices to help teams deliver value efficiently. Examples include Scrum, Kanban, Extreme Programming (XP), and Lean.
Agile Manifesto	A foundational document for software development expressing the core values and principles that inform Agile project management, created in 2001 by 17 software experts.
Agile Principles	Guiding principles that build on and expand the concepts embodied in the Agile values, facilitating the development of an Agile mindset and work practices.

Term	Definition
Agile Values	The core beliefs that guide the Agile methodology, such as prioritizing individuals and interactions over processes and tools, working software over comprehensive documentation, customer collaboration over contract negotiation, and responding to change over following a plan.
Customer Value	The benefit a product delivers to its users. In other words, how well does the software (or solution) meet customer needs and solve their problems?
Epics	Large, high-level requirements that represent major user needs or business capabilities, often spanning multiple sprints.
Events	Time-boxed activities (often called “ceremonies”) that give Scrum its rhythm. They provide regular opportunities for the team to plan, inspect, adapt, and deliver value. Standard Scrum events include the Sprint, Sprint Planning, the Daily Scrum, the Sprint Review, and the Sprint Retrospective.

Term	Definition
Features	Specific functionalities that deliver value to the user and contribute to fulfilling an epic.
Goals	Specific, measurable objectives derived from the vision. Goals translate broad aspirations into actionable outcomes that guide decision-making and prioritization.
Increment	A usable, potentially shippable piece of the product that is produced at the end of each sprint.
Information Radiators	Visual displays (e.g., a task board on the wall, an online Kanban board, or a sprint burndown chart) that broadcast the team's status at a glance. By "radiating" information outward, these tools allow everyone—team members, Scrum Master, Product Owner, and stakeholders—to stay aligned, discuss bottlenecks, and make quick decisions whenever needed.
Just in Time (JIT) Planning	An iterative approach where stakeholders and teams work together to complete a project, planning just enough—a few steps ahead.

Term	Definition
Kanban	An Agile framework that emphasizes lean principles such as continuous delivery, a pull-based workflow system, working on a single piece at a time, limiting work in progress, and visualizing workflow with a Kanban board.
Nonfunctional Requirements	Define how the software should execute the functional requirements. Non-functional requirements relate to the software's quality and performance, such as speed, reliability, usability, security, etc.
Production Environment	The actual environment where the software runs and operates for the customer. The staging environment helps to ensure that the software meets the quality and functionality requirements and that there are no bugs or errors in the production environment.
Scrum	An iterative and lightweight Agile software development framework. It focuses on small teams of people working together with highly specified roles to address complex problems, incrementally deliver value, and continuously improve.

Term	Definition
Scrumban	A hybrid Agile framework that blends the structure and discipline of Scrum with the flexibility and flow of Kanban.
Servant Leadership	A leadership approach where the leader's primary role is to support, empower, and enable their team rather than command or control. A servant leader prioritizes the growth, well-being, and success of the team, removes obstacles, and fosters a culture of trust, collaboration, and continuous improvement.
Software Development Life Cycle (SDLC)	The structured process for developing, testing, deploying, and maintaining software. It typically includes stages like planning, analysis, design, implementation, testing, deployment, and maintenance.
Sprint	Timeboxed intervals of work (typically two weeks) characteristic of Agile frameworks like Scrum.
Sprint Goal	A concise statement that describes the intended outcome of the sprint. It provides direction and focus, helping the team align their efforts while allowing flexibility in how they achieve it.

Term	Definition
Staging Environment	A replica of the production environment where the software can be tested and evaluated before it is released to the customer. The staging environment allows the team to get feedback from the customer and make any changes or improvements before the final release.
Story points	Story points are a relative measure used in Agile to estimate the effort required to complete a task or user story. They consider complexity, effort, and risk, rather than specific time estimates. For example, a simple task might be 1 point, while a complex one could be 8 or more.
Tasks	Actionable steps required to complete a user story, often broken down into technical or design work.
User Stories	Small, user-focused increments of work that describe a specific requirement from the end user's perspective.

Term	Definition
Value	The measurable benefit a product or project provides to both users and the organization. It encompasses meeting customer needs, solving problems effectively, and achieving strategic business objectives, such as revenue growth, cost reduction, or operational efficiency.
Vision	The high-level purpose and long-term aspiration of a project or product. It defines the overarching "why" behind the work, providing direction and inspiration for the team.
Waterfall	The traditional linear project delivery framework. It involves planning, estimating, and documenting a complete solution up front. Its cascading process is like a waterfall, hence the term.

8

References

Beck, Kent, Mike Beedle, Arie van Bennekum, Alistair Cockburn, Ward Cunningham, Martin Fowler, James Grenning, et al. 2001. *Manifesto for Agile Software Development.* https://agilemanifesto.org/.

Digital.ai. 2021. "15th State of Agile Report."

Digital.ai. 2023. "17th State of Agile Report."

Farrier, John. 2024. "Agile Failure – What Drives "268% Higher Failure Rates?"." *John Farrier - For Software Engineers.* 7 June. https://johnfarrier.com/agile-failure-what-drives-268-higher-failure-rates/.

JCURV. 2020. "State of Agile Culture 2020 Report." https://static1.squarespace.com/static/61950fecc213a82f85628df3/t/63da4508f933a151eeb3fcbc/1675248905728/State_Of_Agile_Culture_2020-1+Report.pdf.

Mishra, A., and Y.I. Alzoubi. 2023. "Structured software development versus agile software development: a comparative analysis." *International Journal of Systems Assurance Engineering and Management* 14 (4): 1504–1522. doi:https://doi.org/10.1007/s13198-023-01958-5.

Pavel Naydenov. n.d. *What Is an Agile Organization?* https://businessmap.io/agile/agile-at-scale/agile-organization#:~:text=An%20agile%20organization%20is%20a,continuous%20delivery%20of%20valuable%20products.

Quick, Lindy. 2024. *Top Scrum Case Study Examples in Real-life 2024.* 17 May. https://www.knowledgehut.com/blog/agile/scrum-case-study-examples.

Schwaber, Ken, and Jeff Sutherland. 2020. *Scrumguides.org.* November. Accessed June 22, 2023. https://scrumguides.org/scrum-guide.html#scrum-team.

This page has been left intentionally blank.

This page has been left intentionally blank.

This page has been left intentionally blank.

This page has been left intentionally blank.

This page has been left intentionally blank.

www.ingramcontent.com/pod-product-compliance
Lightning Source LLC
LaVergne TN
LVHW022045200926
848481LV00003B/790

* 9 7 8 0 9 9 4 1 6 9 3 4 1 *